Navy Blue and Gold

Navy Blue and Gold

Boats, Boatels an' all of
FRANK NORTH

AB

AVON BOOKS
1 Dovedale Studios
465 Battersea Park Road
London SW11 4LR

This book has been sold subject to the condition that
it shall not, by way of trade or otherwise, be lent, re-sold,
hired out, photocopied or held in any retrieval system, or otherwise
circulated without the publisher's consent in any
form of binding or cover other than in which this is published
and without a similar condition including this condition
being imposed on the subsequent purchaser.

Printed and bound in the U.K.

Avon Books

London
First Published 1998
© Frank North, 1998
ISBN 1 86033 499 7

Frank North, born in Yorkshire, England, learned to sail in luggers on the West coast of England. He had his own command in the Royal Navy during World War II, and was sailing master for the famed CHARLOTTE RHODES in the BBC series, THE ONEDIN LINE.

Frank North is well known in the sailing world of Great Britain. He built the first two BOATELS in the world at Dartmouth, Devon and in Cawsands, Cornwall. He then moved to Carratraca, Málaga.

The sculptures of fig-wood are from his own finca, made by hand and use the natural bends of trunks and branches of the trees to give movement.

Without any specialised training in the arts, today, Frank North's paintings and sculptures are in private collections around the world ... and his carved figureheads sail the oceans.

Frank North died in 1994.

FRANK NORTH

SPANISH PRESS COMMENTS

José Mayorga de "Sur"

"... San Francisco de Asís, realizada sobre una higuera ... sin cortaria aún ... la ha realizado el artista inglés Frank North, y la talla es realmente admirable, con un acierto muy considerable en su realización. La figura tiene una gran serenidad, que se ha logrado al doter al rostro de unas facciones alargadas -casi góticas- y una penetrante mirada hacia la bondad de la naturaleza que conformó la humana andadura del santo, y que el artista ha sabido interpretar con maestría y oficio."

"... la madera enoblecída por el arte de Frank North"

El Poeta José María Lópera de "Sur"

"El pintor, que ha sido hombre de mar tiene (en sus cuadros) la nostalgia de puertos y de playas, de veleros anclados en riveras tranquilas o surcando olas bravas, como si él mismo quisiera volver a los caminos de todas las distancias ..."

SPANISH PRESS IN ENGLISH

Dom de Leon "Iberian Daily Sun"

"... He's been drawing and carving all his life ... could give lessons on what true art is ... the man's awareness for life and nature ... he's no primitive; there is dimension, scope, depth in his work ..."

"... North's works are sellers, especially his paintings of boats ..."

"... there is beauty unlimited in North's work ..."

GUIDEPOST
SPAIN'S AMERICAN WEEKLY MAGAZINE

Frank North
"The 'authentic' boat painter ..."
"... a boat owner for more years than he cares to remember, a man who has sketched, drawn and painted boats for all those years, even tackled scrimshaw work as well as carving ships' figureheads ..."

BRITISH PRESS IN THE UNITED KINGDOM

"... not all those gaily-painted figureheads you see sprouting from the bows of sailing ships were made by craftsmen of the past." "... one making them today ... Frank North ... Give him a length of timber and he will turn you out a figurehead ... like those masterpieces of the past."

"... Beautifully decorated figureheads carved by him ... he is still 'bringing alive' pieces of dead wood."

Frank North at work in 1966

Chapter 1

The train was just pulling out of Pokesdown Station as I ran across the iron bridge, scuttled down the steps and scrambled into the last carriage. "Only just managed that, me 'andsom," drawled the old feller on the opposite seat.

"I thought it were one o' they Messmittle airyplanes after thee."

I grinned, relaxed and started to fill my pipe. This was the train to Southampton, and before 8:00 a.m. one could buy a 'Workman's' ticket for 1/6 - hence the rush, due also to the fact that I'm always late for everything. At Southampton I walked through the rubble of the previous night's air-raid. I arrived at the Recruiting Office for the second time in two weeks. It was not yet open. Sitting on the top step I thought back on my reasons for my persistent efforts to volunteer.

I was twenty-four years of age and the second World War had been going on for two years. Being employed by the Post Office Engineering Department, I was 'reserved' and fed up with the idea. All my friends were in the armed services. I knew that when eventually I was called up, I would be drafted into the Royal Corps of Signals. Apart from the fact that I didn't know an ohm from a hole in the ground, I wanted to join the Royal Navy, or at least go to sea in some form or another. Two weeks before, I had seen an advertisement in the local newspaper asking for volunteers;

1

fishermen, yachtsmen, ex-Merchant marines etc. To join a new branch being formed by the Royal Air Force - the Air-Sea Rescue Service. "That's for me," says I, so I had a day 'off sick' and applied at these same offices for recruitment into the R.A.F.

After being ushered into the office, I went before the doctor, was stripped, weighed, measured etc. I touched my toes and coughed when asked. My eyes and ears were tested. I filled in a form stating all my antecedents, dressed, and then stood to attention in a smaller room, where, sitting behind a desk was a Wing-Commander with a chest full of medals and a huge moustache. I handed him my papers.

"Mmm, yes," he said, looking at them. "Physically in good shape. So you play rugger. Good! Done a bit of rowing I see, oh, and quite a bit of sailing. Ideal I should think."

I beamed, this was more like it.

"Where do you work, young man?" he said, looking at me rather shrewdly.

"I - er - mm. Er —"

"Well, come on! What sort of job are you doing?"

"I, er - sort of work —!"

"Christ, man! Who employs you?"

"The G.P.O.," I muttered.

He bounced out of his chair, moustache bristling. "Out! Out!" he snarled. "Wasting my bloody time. I thought so! You are in a Reserved Occupation! Out!" he gritted, flinging my paper on to a pile at the side of his desk. "Bloody civilians!"

On my return to work the following day I was hauled over the carpet by the District Engineer for taking time off.

"There is a war on you know, Mr. North!" he snapped. "I've heard that you want to go to sea and I'll do my best for you when the time comes. Now, then, no more days off! Right! - And close the door on the way out!"

Oh well, at least I tried, and he did say he would help me

if he could. But yesterday my call-up papers arrived for the Royal Corps of Signals! Sod it! Hence me having another day off sick!

At 0900 hrs a Chief Petty Officer with a red sash and medals galore turned into my doorway, and alongside me, fumbled for his key to the Reserve Office.

"Hello, young feller," he grinned. "Waiting for a bus?"

"Morning, Chief," I said, "I've come to join the Navy."

"Oh, sorry, Lad," he said, pushing open the door. "We're not taking anyone at present."

I slipped my foot in and squeezed after him into the office. He turned, looking rather surprised.

"I told you, son, we are full up at the moment - we are not looking for anyone."

"Chief - we've got the biggest navy in the world - surely you can take one more?"

"Look, lad," he said, "you just don't walk into the Royal Navy. You have forms to fill in. You've got ta 'ave a medical. Get y'r eyes and ears tested. Teeth - the lot. Sorry, young man."

"Chief," I said, sliding across the room, "I was in here," opening the door to the R.A.F. Office, "two weeks ago."

I bent down alongside the R.A.F. desk.

"I had a medical and filled in all my forms, and" - I was shuffling away at the pile of papers - "Here's mine!" I said, holding them out to the astonished C.P.O.

"You're a saucy young sod," he said, flipping through the papers.

"I'm not really, Chief," I said placatingly, - "but all my all life I've wanted to join the Royal Navy, and this is the last chance I'm going to get!"

He nodded, looking through the papers.

"Aye - got a boat of yer own I see, eh? Ever sail a Montague Whaler?"

"Yes," I said, "twenty seven feet long, 6 ft. 3 inch beam of yawl-rigged - really a pulling boat, but with that big centre-board it goes to windward a treat!"

He beamed.

"I was Captain's cox'n on the old *Malaya* in 1934. Won the Home Fleet Cup we did in our Whales. The skipper filled it four times with champers. Bless 'im!"

He became serious again and put on a pair of steel-rimmed glasses, which changed him from a tough old sea-dog to a kindly old gentleman.

"Aye, lad, but there's another snag 'ere. Everyone 'oo joins these days 'as to 'ave a per-si-colojy test."

"What's that?"

"Oh, er, per-si-colojy is, er, well, we've all got to 'ave 'em, and I know our young lady what does 'em is going to Shaftesbury today, and it's no use —"

The door clicked open, interrupting him, and a pretty Wren officer in a tricorne hat popped her head into the room.

"Chief," she said, "I'm on my way to the station - got to get to Shaftesbury - remember? My train goes in twenty minutes."

"Miss, could you do this young man before you go? - He's dead keen!"

"We-ell," she said, looking down at her watch, "I haven't much time."

"I don't need much time, m'am," I chipped in, giving her my toothiest grin.

She started to shake her head, then gave me a pretty smile.

"All right," she said. "You must hurry, though" - and tried to look severe and all Navy Blue and Gold.

She flipped a couple of foolscap questionnaires onto the table.

"Come along, young man - chop! chop!"

Scribbling quickly, I picked out all the easiest questions.

"How high is a tall hat? If not, why not? How many sides to an octagon?" - As if I cared.

"Have you finished, young man?"

"Just a sec!"

"Why does a freeze burst a water pipe?"

"Can't wait any longer - sign your name at the bottom of the paper!"

"It's very good of you, m'am," I said. "It does mean a lot to me, joining the Navy."

"Not at all," she said severely. "This is my job." Then her eyes twinkled, "I know how you feel, though. My Dad and my brother are both in the Service - Mom would be too if she had the chance. Best of luck Mr. —er North," looking at the signature. "And the Best of British! Bye Chief, see you about six, yes?" And she was gone.

I turned to the older man - he was grinning all over his face.

"What now?" I said, mopping my brow.

"Now, lad, you're in the Andrew!" (Royal Reserves for R.N.)

"Eh?"

"You're in the Royal Navy," he explained the Navyese.

"Are you sure of that, Chief?"

"Sure I'm sure," he chortled.

"Well now," I said, "I'll tell you something. Up to this morning, I was in the Royal Corps of Signals, but I sent my papers back and said I wasn't coming, I was in the Royal Navy!"

"Saucy young bugger," he said approvingly, "but fer Gawd's sake, watch out fer they Red Caps. - You'll be in the bloody glass-house if they catch you. I'll put your papers through today - you should get them in about a week. Right! Best of luck to you young feller - it's the finest service in the world - bar none!"

Bless his old heart, I agree with him!

Chapter 2

Walking back home that evening from the bus stop, I had a big silly grin on my face. I'd done it! I was in the Royal Navy and couldn't believe my luck! Ever since I was a small boy I had wanted to go to sea, but somehow circumstances had always prevented it.

Born in Leeds, Yorkshire, from the age of five I had trudged 'snail-like unwillingly' twice daily through the slush, two miles across the poppy field, over the slag heaps. Squeeze through the railing (always late) to my Alma Mater - Cross Flatts Park Council school, known laughingly as an Elementary School. All I remember of those days was the cold, northern winters, ugh! The snow and the slush reaching my knees, sticking out of short pants. They were always red and chapped with the cold. Little boys didn't wear long trousers in those days until they left school at fourteen years of age when they were 'britched'. Jeans were worn only by plumbers and then they were called overalls.

Tall for my age, I had lank brown hair with a fringe, wore old fashioned boots (steel protectors fore & aft), hand-knitted socks usually drooping over my ankles, had a constant sniff and usually a runny nose. Needless to say, I was very self-conscious. Every Christmas I asked for a pair of "Wellies" but didn't get them. My mother would pull out a pair of heavy socks over my boots "keep out the cold". Useless, of course. Ten minutes of slush and they were wet through and my feet made even more cold. I would rush to the cast iron hot water pipes of the school room to steam-dry out my wet pants. I always burned my bum too.

Mathematics was unheard of at Cross Flatts School. I was taught arithmetic (which I hated). The algebra master had a nasty trick of pulling me up from my seat by the short hairs on the back of my neck. He scared me stiff! My only good subject was drawing; composition was passable. When weighed up, the only part I really liked about school was the holidays.

In summer I would stay with my Aunt Annie in Lincolnshire. She was my father's only sister, but he had ignored her for many years. She was a widow, and 'living with a man'. Her husband had died in his thirties, leaving her a son, who was fourteen years older than me. Cousin Bill had a weak chest and the doctor had said, unless he left the smoke and grime of industrial Leeds he would never survive. Ernest Dring, a draughtsman, had loved my aunt for many years. His own wife was in a mental asylum and didn't even recognise him. Ernest was one of the kindest men I had ever known. He took my aunt and her son to live in the country, with a job as a pigman. They all went to live on Pyewyke Farm between Waddingham and Redburn. Bill started work too, as a farmboy. Their home was on the edge of a big wood, they had a deep well for drinking water and paraffin lamps for lighting. The family's big old collie dog was called Tick. When I couldn't be found, I would eventually be discovered asleep in Tick's kennel.

Bill had been promoted to 'Waggoners' when I first went there. He would get me out of bed at about six-thirty in the morning and carry me across the dew-wet fields to the stables. Lighting an old oil lamp, he worked on the horses, rubbing them down, curry-combing and feeding them, and all the time talking to them in his broad Yorkshire accent. They would nuzzle into his open shirt front for the crusts of bread he had hidden there. The horses were huge, eighteen hand shires, each weighing about a ton, big gentle beasts with great hairy legs and an enormous capacity for work. The shires were named Governor, Bluebell, Nap, General, and my favourite, Captain. I would sit on his back with my legs sticking out sideways while Bill did the mucking-out.

No matter how cold the weather, it was always warm in the stables with the body heat of the animals. The air smelled of hay, apples, wine, leather, meat and paraffin. Bill would wrap me in an old khaki overcoat, harness Captain and Bluebell to a great wooden cart with iron-shod wheels, trundle off to Brigg market with a load of potatoes or sugar beet, stopping at Redbourne for a cup of tea and a sticky Bath bun.

My August holiday was harvest time, and in the 40 acre field six great horses drew three binders, which cut the corn, scooped it up, tied it in bundles with coarse white string and tossed it aside. The machines had been invented many years before but could not be marketed until a gadget was developed that could tie a knot in the twine. Even when this was achieved, the sheaves, rolling off the side, had to be stooked by hand in clumps of eight. Round and round the field the horses went, hour by hour, in a haze of golden dust. Word would pass around the village, "They'll be finishin' off t' Forty-Acre s'afternoon," and men and boys would make their way to the field, each carrying a nobbly stick or a shotgun - all had dogs with them.

As the area of growing corn grew smaller and smaller, the rabbits hiding there would make a bolt for it, and men, boys, and dogs would go scrambling after them yelling and shouting. It was all great fun for me to watch. In those pre-war days a man was lucky to have a job at two pounds a week, and a rabbit would provide a meal for a small family. The womenfolk came along later with beer or cider, or, more often, bottles of cold tea, plus thick sandwiches and home-made scones.

At day's end, Bill would unharness the horses and put me on Captain's fat shiny back, dropping me off at the cottage on the way home. My legs and arms would be scratched with stooking, face red and peeling with the sun, and I was always covered with midge-bites, called locally Harvest Bugs. Aunt Annie would dab me with vinegar and water, tuck me into bed in cool hand-washed sheets, and I'd be fast asleep before Bill had even watered his charges.

One summer, however, was different and stands out in memory. My Dad must for once have backed a winner. He took my mother, my sister, and me to the seaside for a week's holiday. At that period in history, Scarborough was as much a fishing port as a holiday resort. We stayed at Mrs. Topham's boarding house on the prom. I had cried the night of arrival with a nasty earache. Mom said,

"Harry, lad, the sun is just coming up - tek ar Frank for a walk on the front - it'll give him something else to think about."

We dressed, then Dad and I walked down the prom to the harbour. The herring fleet was putting out to sea. The Scots fisher girls were already working - they were a braw bunch o' lasses. Arms bared above the elbows, rough and reddened with the salt and wind, knives flashing. Their hands moved with lightning speed cutting the cold slippery fish. They shrieked, laughing and talking in a language of their own, exchanging shouts with the fishermen gliding past in their black tarred sailing luggers.

Many years later I made a study of these lovely fishing boats. There were Scaffies, Fifies & Zulus from Scotland with huge loose-footed dipping lugsails and forward raking mizzens. Ketch-rigged smacks from the East Coast, drifters from the Isle of Man; nobbies and cutters from Lancashire, with long, unstayed bowsprits and not an engine to be seen. Each year they followed the herring shoals down the east coast from Scotland to Cornwall. Thousands of people were employed in the industry, boat-builders, sailmakers, coopers, fishermen as well as hundreds of fishergirls.

Clinging to Father's hand I watched the boats disappear into the distance. Hundreds of tanned brown sails, gliding out between the harbour walls until, like floating leaves, they vanished into the fine mist. It was the only time I ever saw them in such numbers, and I'll never forget the sight of those boats - even then I wanted to paint a picture of them. Oh, the smells and sights I saw that morning! Of course, by the time we got back for breakfast - porridge, kippers, toast and marmalade, and lots of cups of strong tea - I had forgotten my earache. Mum was right, as usual.

Chapter 3

My father was an inveterate gambler, as were his father and grandfather before him. Grandfather at one time owned a public house at Kirkstall near Leeds. It was called the 'Star and Garter'. One day he put the pub as it stood, lock stock and barrel on a greyhound he had bred himself, then entered it in the Waterloo Cup - the number one correct event of the year. The greyhound lost by a nose. Sadly, he turned to Grandma, saying, "Come on, Sarah, lass, leave everything except your delftware and pewter plates, they belonged to thy Mother." Then they just walked out forever. No one seems to have recorded Grandma's words but she was a lady and maybe said nowt. The Delft, as it was called, was an old Yorkshire dresser with a plate-rack upon which were these lovely pewter plates. According to stories my mother told, my forebears lived at Cookridge Hall, a beautiful sandstone house near Adel Church on the outskirts of Leeds. My ancestors are buried near the fine Norman doorway. I was told of the pretty, wilful daughter of the house who ran away with the family groom, was cut off with a shilling and left with only her clothing and the Delft with its pewter plates which she had inherited from her grandmother.

As a matter of interest, one hundred years later I visited Kirkstall and spent some time browsing around a mock-up of the old village in the Abbey Museum. This was very well-conceived with old shops, a bakery, a blacksmith's forge with all its implements, and a carpenter's workshop. On the lid of the toolbox I remember was the late tradesman's name, William N. Limb. Later I inquired of the curator the whereabouts of the one-time Star and Garter Inn. He had never heard of the place, but an old gaffer who was listening to the conversation told me where it was. Eventually I found this rather nice, stone-built edifice alongside the arched bridge over the River Aire. It was the 'Star and Garter' no longer, alas, but was converted into a discotheque called the 'Bar-Celona'. Gone to the dogs again!

Chapter 4

My father was tall and thin, with a fantastic sense of humour. A very kindly person he was, and known as a compulsive gambler. He had served in the Northumberland Fusiliers in the First World War, classed medically at C3 (the lowest category), but as he played the fiddle he spent his war years playing in the Band of the Officers' Mess. At the cessation of hostilities he started again in business as a bespoke tailor. He had a fine reputation as a craftsman, but unfortunately for the rest of the family, he was no businessman, and every penny he made went on the horses.

He had a friend called John Willie Fox, a night telephonist at Leeds Exchange. This of course was many years before automatic phones. Dad would sally forth nightly to the South Leeds Conservative Club to contact John Willie, who spent his evenings listening to all the bookies' calls, and conversations between trainers and jockeys. Usually he had on hand a dead cert. on which Father would plonk all his daily takings. He invariably lost the lot. My father died of cancer in his forty-fifth year, when I was seven. Mother was left with a shop packed with boxes empty of goods, a mortgaged house, and no money. None at all! Dad had always stated flatly he didn't believe in insurance. The next door neighbour was a carpenter and undertaker, William Limb. He kindly took matters out of Mother's hands for the funeral. She confessed that she just hadn't any money. He replied, "Mrs. North, when I send in my account - that will be the time for you to worry about paying." The account was never sent. The name I remember well. W. N. Limb.

Our little family of three now moved up Dewsbury Road, and rented an old house where Mother took in lodgers. My sister, Nancy, who was seven years older than me, got a job at the G.P.O. as a probation telephonist, earning 8/- a week. I still went to Cross Flatts School, my drawing and painting improved, but not my arithmetic. When I was thirteen years of age I captained the school Rugby League team and also played for the city boys. My name would appear (in very small letters) in the sports column of the Yorkshire Evening Post. Fame at last! When the town team played at home, their opponents, Wigan, St. Helens, and Wakefield, would bring along a team of their schoolboys to play a game before the big match to keep the spectators happy. The lads from Lancashire, not having any football boots, wore their usual brass-bound clogs. The mothers who came with them, dressed in shawls and men's caps, would encourage their offspring with such cries as "Clog 'm, Jimmy!" or "Give 'im some iron, lad!" After this lot we were allowed to watch the main game for nothing.

The day before I left school at the age of fourteen, I was interviewed by the Headmaster regarding my future. He peered over steel-rimmed spectacles, and sighed, saying, "What would you like to do for a living, North?"

"I would like to make stained-glass windows, sir," I said promptly.

"Stained-glass? You're daft, lad! What's wrong wi' t' Pit? How much a week do you think you'll make at that job - stained-glass?"

Not having any idea, I got a faraway look in my eye and said, "Er - five pounds a week, sir."

He shook his head sadly, "Ee, lad, that's more than I get - you've no idea at all, have you? Off you go!"

That was the only 'advice' I ever received regarding taking employment.

Unemployment was rife in those days, and I was lucky to get a first job as a flour boy in the grocery department of Leeds Industrial Co-operative Society (Co-op). Bags of flour were hoisted to the top floor of the building, whereupon the contents were sent down a wooden chute to the bottom floor (I'll never know why). A paper bag was then held in front of the sliding tin lid, the idea being that the said flour would gently fill it, but with about 70 foot of the stuff pushing down the chute, this was a bit much and, when the flap was opened even one half inch, the whole room was covered in flour. Me an' all!

It was also my job to deliver groceries to our various customers, my only means of transport being a trolley with small cast iron wheels upon which would be stacked five or six boxes of groceries, the whole being (in theory) held in position by a piece of hairy string. The streets locally were cobbled and time and again I would hit a pothole and over would go the groceries. "Ee, lad, my butter was right mucky last week," a housewife would say. Considering that I'd had to scrape it off the pavement it wasn't surprising. One place to which I delivered was the Griffin Hotel in Boon Lane. I considered this very posh and I was always given three pence tip. However, I did enjoy the job of feeding the Co-op cat. Daily I visited the L.I.C.S. restaurant to collect a bagful of lovely fried fish - which I promptly ate! There were perks to the job too. With a wire I could cut a quarter-inch slice of whole cheese without its being noticed. I would gobble it down, and finish it off with a couple of handfuls of nuts and raisins. Well - I was a growing lad wasn't I? However, I felt somehow that this really wasn't me. So, when my Auntie Hilda and Uncle Bill decided to start a boarding-house in Blackpool, asking my Mother to join them as cook, I was just delighted!

Chapter 5

Our bits of furniture (including the Delft) were piled on an open lorry, with yours truly wrapped in a blanket, sitting in an armchair. I was violently sick from all the exhaust fumes so it wasn't a very happy journey. We crossed the Pennines, and about midnight we arrived at a cold empty building smelling of wet plaster and new paint. Ugh! It was going to be called 'Leeds House' would you believe - very original! The following morning, hearing a strange booming sound I asked, "What's that noise, mum?"

"Ooh, love, it's the sea breaking on the beach - isn't it champion? I'm sure we shall all like living in Blackpool."

Later that morning the plumber arrived to fix the gas stove, and Mother promptly asked him if he could do with a strong hand to help him. He thought about it for a minute, then said, "Yes - tell him to come around to the workshop in the morning, and I'll start him off at 7/6 a week. And he'll get a week off every year with pay - What about that?" That was the law, so he wasn't being very generous.

"Ee, ow, Frank," Mom said, beaming, "aren't you lucky? You've got a job in the building trade - and no matter what happens - people will always need a plumber."

"Too right!"

I turned up at the workshop the next morning (five minutes late, of course). "We start 'ere at 8:00 a.m., lad," said the boss - "And don't forget it. And get rid of that school cap and get a proper 'at!"

Well, clothes maketh the man!

"Grab 'old o' that 'andcart to start with, lad," I was told. It was just a flat cart with iron-shod wooden wheels and a six foot handle at the back. The other workman put on a thirty foot extending ladder so I was five feet behind the vehicle load to start with. A large crate of glass was stuck on top, a drum of putty, three coils of lead pipes, tools, paint-pots and assorted iron work.

"Nah then, you know wheer t' Gynne is?"

"No, I only arrived here yesterday," I said hopefully, gazing at the load on the cart.

"Well, thee'll find it. Go over Bloomfield Road bridge. Keep on till tha comes to the prom. Turn right and keep going and you'll come to 'Uncle Tom's Cabin'. It's a big pub - tha can't miss it. Turn down first road out right - ask for Bill Snapes buildings - and don't be long. Off thee goes!"

Well, the wheels were already four inches down in the mud so I had to have a push to get started. Bloomfield Road bridge was about 1 in 6 and a couple of chaps gave me a hand to push the load up and over. Going down the other side I went like a train of course - I couldn't stop! Straight across the tram lines at the bottom, and there was a great clanging of bells as two tram cars pulled up smartly to let me pass. I hit the promenade at about 5 knots and it was only the wind shrieking in from the sea that stopped me from a ducking. It must have been about four and a half miles to 'Uncle Tom's Cabin', pushing hard against a force seven. I then turned right but couldn't find the building plot.

"Ee, lad - tha should've turned at 'Lectric Bobbies - tha can see it from theer," said an old geezer standing close by. ('Lectric Bobbies was the name for the new-fangled traffic lights installed by Lord Belisha, the then Minister of Transport.) It was 12:20 when I returned to the workshop. I was duly admonished for "takin' all the bloody morning" and was allowed only half an hour for lunch.

However, I liked living in Blackpool. As Mother had said, "What boy wouldn't?" There was so much to do and see. The Tower with its Zoo, variety theatre and things going on all the time. The Golden Mile had lots of freak shows, ice cream and hokey-pokey stands, and more ways of extracting the pennies from your pocket than the parson could preach about. The Illuminations, called in Lancashire - T'Leets, were quite fantastic. I'd never seen anything like them before. The vast amusement park on the South Shore with its huge roller coaster, music stands where one could sing and enjoy the comedians, and all for nothing! Swings, chairoplanes, roundabouts. For two pence I went on the North Pier, fishing for dabs and eels and flounders. I joined the Blackpool Sea Scouts - it was much more interesting than scouting in Leeds. Our troop had been given a whaler. We scouts spent weeks burning off and painting it. Then when all was done, we learned how to row. We had no rig but we hoped that later on we should be able to sail it.

A strange little incident occurred a short while after we moved into Leeds House. My mother, nattering (kalling) over the garden wall with the next-door neighbours, discovered that they were spiritualists and held a little séance in the evening with their friends - perhaps she would like to join them some night? The next evening she and my sister accepted this invitation. After settling down, a hymn was sung and all joined in a short prayer. The husband was the medium, and in the darkened room he went into a trance. There was silence, then the unmistakable voice of my father said, "Hello, Annie, love - Hello, Sprodger. So you've come to live in Blackpool then! It's a bit of a change from Leeds isn't it?"

Mother was petrified! Nancy burst into tears. The only person who had called her Sprodger had been my father.

Continuing, the voice said, "You will all like it here, especially 'ar Mick - he'll love it."

My Dad's nickname for me had always been Mickey Dripping - or Mick for short - just one of those family things.

"But Annie, love," said the voice, "you won't be here for very long - you are all going eventually to live in Wakefield." This was after being only two or three weeks in Blackpool. Wakefield was only a town we had passed through on the train on visits to Lincolnshire. It didn't mean anything to us. After oohing and aahing we forgot the foretelling.

One day, working on a rooftop fixing lead chimney flashings I was mate to a chap called Stanley Woods. "Wot's this I 'ear, Frankie," he said. "You've joined Sea Scouts. After that you'll be joining the Royal Navy, eh? Can you sail a boat?"

"Not yet," I said seriously, "but we've done a bit of rowing on Stanley Park Lake."

"Well that's better than most, innit? Do you like mucking about in boats, then?"

"Yes, I do an' all," I said. "And wot's more - one day I'm going to have a boat of my own, big enough to live on - and time to sail it."

"Then what?"

"Well — er — I'll sail around the world and paint pictures!"

"Well, you won't make any brass painting pictures, lad - but if it's what you want to do - well, you're not going to get rich as a plumber either! Eh, pass those bloody wedges - we'll be 'ere all day!"

We worked quietly for five minutes.

"Franky."

"Yes."

"You think all boat owners are millionaires like Tommy Lipton, don't you? You know, the Lipton's Tea chap that owns *Shamrock*?"

"Wait a minute! *Shamrock* is that big 'J' Class cutter that was trying to win the Yankees' Cup. I've got it in my scrapbook."

"That's right! You know your boats, don't you?"

"Well, if I see anything about sailing boats in the papers, I cut it out and stick it in my scrapbook."

"Do you now? That's interesting - good idea!"

"Why Stan - have you a boat, or summat?" I said with a grin.

"Well, as a matter o' fact I have."

"Give over! What sort is it - a rowing boat?"

"No," he said, putting down his hammer and chisel and looking at me.

"It's a thirty-six foot nobby - does that mean owt to you?"

"A nobby? A Lancashire nobby? Yes, it is one of those cutter-rigged fishing boats that sails out of Fleetwood - catching shrimps! Right?"

"That's right," he said. "She's called the *Two Brothers*. She's thirty feet long and I gave twenty-eight quid for her. I've been converting her into a yacht for three years. My brother used to help me - it's the name that attracted us in the first place - but he's got a bit of frippet now and has lost interest. I could do with a hand now and again though." Silence.

"Stan."

"What?"

"Er - where do you keep your boat?"

"Over at Skipool - it's about seven miles from here - I go over every night on my bike, take a couple of sandwiches and make a cup of tea when I get there."

"Have you got a stove on board then?"

"'Course I have - a proper galley. Saloon, coal-stove, bunks, water tanks - the lot. I tell you, I've been working on her for three years."

"Ooh!" I came up like a starving trout for a fly.

"Stan."

"What now?"

"Could I come over and see her some time? Er - you know - just to have a look, like?"

"I don't see why not," he said, grinning.

That was my introduction to a sailing boat, the real love of my life.

I had read of Alan Villiers' voyage on the *Grace Howar* and, later, his book *By Way of Cape Horn* on the *Joseph Conrad*. I read *The Cruise of the Amaryllis* by Mulhauser, the *Riddle of the Sands*, in fact any book I could find in the library on sailing. Racing or sailing yachts with their long sleek hulls I didn't aspire to, only working boats that could be picked up for very little in those days, when an engine was a luxury and not a necessity and the virtues of gaff and Bermudan rig were still being hotly discussed or argued about in the yachting periodicals. The *Two Brothers* was a typical nobby, a Morecambe Bay prawner, thirty-six feet long with a high straight stem shelving away to a low elliptical stern. Built at Arnside in Northumberland to dredge over the shoals for prawns, which, when caught, were boiled in a copper over a wood or coal fire and landed, ready for sale at Fleetwood in the mouth of the River Wyre.

I got to know the Wyre very well. It is not really a pretty stretch of water, but I thought in those days it was beautiful. The estuary must be three quarters of a mile across, narrowing gradually inland through wide mud banks. The range of tide is some twenty-eight feet at springs. The incoming tide races between the banks, and, as it is squeezed, it forms a bore, a small wall of water building up faster and higher as it travels up river. I thought then that this was normal in all rivers, and, at fifteen years of age, I gaily sailed this heavy, hard-mouthed engine-less old cutter in and out of the mudbanks, the only navigational aids being poles with tin cans perched on top, stuck into the mud to mark each mud-spit. Stan, brewing up below decks, would stick his head out of the hatch now and again just to keep his eye on things and test with his fingers the mackerel lines towing astern.

I continued attending weekly meetings of the Sea Scouts. The assistant Scout master was a young chap called John Illingworth, a tall slim fellow with blond, curly hair, who was a partner in the family florist business. From somewhere he had learned of the coming up for sale of an eighty-foot Fleetwood, the *Lord Marmion*, a big ketch, rather like a Brixham trawler. He reckoned she could be had for about thirty pounds complete with fishing gear, thirty-foot greenheart beam trawl, nets, floats, and all the bits and bobs to go with it. Thirty pounds! Let's have a go! He put up the money, the troop held raffles, organized whist drives, sold scent cards for three pence each, held jumble sales and did all we could to pay off his loan. She had no engine, but that, it was decided, could come later. We scraped and painted, caulked decks, stripped down the rigging, and (under instruction) replaced it. We dreamed dreams — and then —

Then, out of the blue came a letter from a long-time girlfriend of my mother's, who lived in the Merrie Cittie, as Wakefield was called three hundred years ago. She suggested that Wakefield, being the centre of West Riding, offered good opportunities for anyone who cared to start a boarding-house - in other words, a good place for lodgers. I was then coming up to sixteen years. We remembered the words from the séance. Was it just coincidence? We went to Wakefield.

Chapter 6

Wakefield! Ugh! I didn't like it a bit. The town then was the centre of the wool industry, surrounded by coal mines and factories. It sat in a hollow with a foggy ball of smoke over it. Everything had a thick coat of soot. I would walk along the banks of the canal, looking at the barges, wondering how the boys were getting on with the old smack and thinking about Stan Woods and the *Two Brothers*, and of the sea and boats. I soon got a job as a plumber's lad again, and from the day I started I was called Young Blackpool. Joe Woodhead, the boss, was a Town Councillor, J.P. and a Committee Member of Wakefield Trinity Rugby League Club. The workshop was in Charlotte Street and employed a staff of about 15 journeymen and improvers. As the newest arrival I was general dogsbody, teaboy and the butt of every practical joke.

On my first day I was told by the foreman to get the handcart and fetch two dozen 9" x 3" pot-logholes from the builders' merchants in Ings Road.

"Where's that?" I said, "I've only just come to live here."

"Tha'll find it, lad," I was told. "Ask anybody - and don't tek all bloody day either."

Off goes Young Blackpool with his handcart clattering over the cobbles and, after trundling the damn thing halfway around the town, I found Ings Road and eventually the builders' merchants. The shop was crowded with men of the building trade and, surprisingly, when I walked in they opened up and politely waved me to the counter.

"Yes, lad," the assistant said smiling. "What can I do for you?"

"I've come from Mr. Woodhead's and I want two dozen pot-logholes 9" x 3"."

"Have you got a handcart, young man? They're pretty heavy."

"Yes," I said.

"Wait a minute, matey - I'll just go and check."

A couple of minutes later he came back looking very apologetic.

"Sorry, me old son," he said, "we're sold out - we've only got $4\frac{1}{2}$" x 3". Will they do?"

"Nay," said a big bricklayer putting his hand on my shoulder. "Don' be daft - Old Joe wouldn't use those. Send 'im down to Enoch's - ee's got some, sure to 'ave." Turning to me he said kindly, "It's quite a way to Enoch's - but if you go up Kirk Gate and past Gas Oose anybody will tell you - and good luck, lad!"

"Thank you, mister," I said, "I'll find it."

Of course, as soon as I had left the place the man behind the counter picked up the phone and, hushing the crowd of delighted customers, said, "Is that thee, Enoch? Aye - well there's a daft lad coming from Joe Wood'ead's with a handcart for some pot-log'oles - send 'im on to Fred 'Andacker's when you've 'ad your fun."

Well, I didn't get back until after dinner-time and I hadn't been able to find a single one! By the way, a pot-loghole is the space left when a brick is knocked out of an existing wall and a pot-log, a 6" x 3" piece of wood, is inserted in its place, the other end being lashed to a scaffold pole. Ah me!

A few weeks later the firm had a job at the Town Hall. A fine stone building, black with many years of soot and smoke, built around a big courtyard with all the municipal offices facing into it. The brickwork needed painting on the fourth floor. Extending ladders were lashed together which took four or five men to hoist into place. An attraction for staff of the offices.

"Now, lad," I was told, "tek this 'ere raking chisel and a big 'ammer, rake out a joint about there" - pointing upwards. "And drive in this iron bar to hold these planks and make a scaffold. Right."

It seemed an 'ell of a way up to me, but sticking a lump hammer in my belt, a raking chisel in my pocket and the pointed iron bar (about 4 feet long, 3 inches wide and 3/8th of an inch thick) in one hand I clambered up the swaying ladder. About 60 feet from the ground I curled my leg around a rung, to hold myself and leave my hands free. I raked out the joint, then hammered the iron bar about 9 inches into the stonework.

"Right, Blackpool," came the charge-hand's voice - "now sit ont' bugger and mek sure it's safe."

I straddled the iron bar with my back pressed against the wall and bounced up and down a time or two. "It's fine, Charley," I shouted.

"Champion!" he said, removing the ladder and standing back. I was petrified. The thin iron bar was rammed up into my crotch and my back and neck were flattened against the wall. Glancing down I could see four or five grinning faces looking up at me and the concrete yard seemed a very long distance away. By now the office girls were leaning out the windows calling "shame".

"Eh Fatty, give that poor kid 'is ladder back," one shouted indignantly. "Poor little sod, he'll fall and break 'is flipping neck!"

"It's all right, missus," yelled the chargehand. "He's got to learn the trade - if he did fall he'd be no bloody good in the building business anyway. Har! Har! Har!"

I was up there on the wall for about twenty minutes, like a fly stuck on a flypaper, feeling very scared and very, very sore. Heigh Ho! The plumber, the handyman in winter and in summer!

The firm of Woodhead's had the contract to do the repair work for Patton & Baldwin's wool mills. I discovered that my adventure stuck high and dry on a wall was less than some poor sods had to suffer. The mill-girls were a tough bunch of cookies - they had one fixed rule: any new boy employed in the mill had to be initiated. At dinner time (not lunch hour, the expression used for the same meal south of the Trent), the poor lad was grabbed by half a dozen of these harpies, taken down to the wool-packing shed and stripped of his trousers. Four of the girls would hold him down whilst another inserted his poor little limp penis into an empty beer bottle. Then one of them would slowly take off her upper garments until she stood naked from the waist upwards. Of course the victim would get an erection forcing the air out of the bottle. With screams of delight and suitable unprintable expressions they would scamper off with his trousers, leaving him there, perhaps for a couple of hours until nature allowed him to take off the bottle.

Chapter 7

New to the town and not knowing anyone, I made a few enquiries then joined the local Scout Troop. There I met a chap with a very friendly grin. He was called Georgie Lifton, and we got on famously, our friendship lasting over fifty years. We went camping and cycling together. He introduced me to the Rugby Club Union. George, a couple of years older than me, was already articled to a civil engineer. He was always a little better than me at everything we did, he ran faster, tackled harder, and he could read and write and count figures. When we chatted up a couple of birds he always managed to get the prettier. We went caving and climbing together on the moors - it was often dangerous, but with Old Georgie on the end of the rope I always felt much happier. One Saturday we cycled up to North Yorkshire and stayed at the youth hostel in Kettlewell costing 1/6 per night. Early the following morning we went over to Alum Pot, one of the most famous underground caves in Yorkshire. We put on our equipment, hob-nailed boots and boiler suits, and proceeded to climb about three hundred feet down a series of swaying rope ladders which someone had conveniently left there. It was as black as pitch, of course, so at the bottom we lit our old paraffin lamps and tied ourselves together with clothes lines - all we could afford. We crawled, walked and wriggled along wet passages and cracks in the rocks, sometimes up to our waists in water, using our flashlights as little as possible to conserve the batteries.

Eventually we crawled into a huge cavern - the size of a cathedral. Enormous stalagmites reared up to the roof with stalactites sixty feet long swooping down over our heads. It was a wonderland with the wet limestone changing colour and shimmering at every movement of our lamps. Water was cascading all around us. It was quite frightening, as all the streams joined together and roared down a vast bottomless cavern about three feet away. No doubt modern caving buffs with their sophisticated equipment would tend to sneer at our efforts, but I was scared and awe-struck at the sheer magnificence. Crawling back against the stream both our lamps went out. We reached the bottom of the rope ladder eventually by the light of one flickering torch. Perhaps we would be considered foolhardy, but we were proud of our accomplishment. Our euphoria was dampened by pouring rain that accompanied our 80 mile bike ride back to Wakefield. But it had been a grand weekend!

Chapter 8

My sister Nancy taught me to dance. Taking up the rug in the kitchen, and to the strains of Nat Gonella and Henry Hall on our 2-valve radio set, we did our 1-2-3, 1-2-3 until she at last decided that I could do it without breaking too many of my future partners' toes. My savings bought my first evening suit from the 'Fifty Shilling' tailors, and a couple of weeks later I was all dressed up and raring to go at the Annual Rugby Club Dance.

"Ee, our Frank," said Mum, "I wish your Dad could see you now. You look right nice in that black suit. But, do you have any money, love?" I had about 2/-. Fumbling in her apron she said, "Here, lad - you must have something for your pocket. Take this half-a-crown, but don't spent it unless you have to, will you?" The dance was a great success, and during the course of the evening I made the acquaintance of and danced with a tall, slender blonde in a beautiful backless evening gown. "Gosh," I thought, "in that outfit she looks like a film star." I had previously seen her at the Rugby Club, laughing and talking to her friends, sons of local mill owners, professional people and the upper crust of the district. (Upper crust - just a lot of crumbs stuck together?) I had always thought she was lovely but had never summoned up enough nerve to make myself known.

Remember, this was the 30's. The majority of the young men in the Rugby Club were at the local Grammar School, and some at the university. They spent more on beer nightly than I earned in a week. George was articled to a civil engineer and had a good education - he was my *entrada* (Spanish for entrance or admission). Unknown to me, my mother and sister who knew more about these things than me had got into the habit of saying that "Frank was studying to be a Sanitary Engineer." This, through exams, city and guilds etc. could be achieved at night school. Many of the town's young business people had learned their trade by starting on the shop floor.

The dance finished. On the way back to her table she said, "My name's Molly."

"Frank," I said.

"I know," she replied, "Frank North - you play for the First Fifteen, you work for Joe Woodhead, and you come from Blackpool. Yes?"

I grinned and squeezed her hand and she squeezed back, her eyes twinkling. She was delightful! Walking her home I wondered if I dared kiss her. We came to the doorway of her house. I hesitated - then, she suddenly stood on tiptoe, slipped her hands around my neck, gave me a big warm kiss, giggled, and said in exaggerated broad Yorkshire "Get off me foot - 'ere's me da" - opened the door and slipped inside. I laughed for sheer joy, turned and walked chuckling down the road. Don't know what she meant by "Get off me foot" and there was certainly no sign of her dad - but who cared! I was in love for the first time!

George was grinning all over his face when I met him the following evening at the Stafford Arms - the rugby crowd's hangout.

"What's on then, North?" he said. "Chatting up Molly Steele last night, were you? Bloody monkey! We've all been working on her since she left school but we've never got anywhere. What is it that you've got - that Blackpool charm?"

"Nay, George lad - she nobbut after me brass. It's me 50 bob suit that gets 'em!"

Molly, I discovered, was the only daughter of the biggest building contractor in the district and Joe Woodhead subcontracted to him. Would you believe?

"What shall I do now, George?" I said. "I didn't arrange to meet her again - I didn't have time."

"Give her a ring lad - get on the blower - ask her to the pictures - there's nowt wrong in that."

It seems incredible now, but I was eighteen and a half years of age and never before had I used a telephone! I went into the telephone box (why not?) and carefully read the instructions:

1   Ask the operator for the number you require.
2   Wait for the ringing tone.
3   Place two pennies in the slot.
4   When you hear the voice at the other end and not before - Press button A.
5   If it's the wrong number, press button B, and you'll get your money back.

Couldn't go wrong, could I? Not for two pence!
Her mother answered the phone.
"Could I speak to Molly, please?"
"What name shall I say, young man?"
"Er, F-F-Frank North."
"Oh."
I didn't like the sound of that "oh", the way she said it.

"Hang on a moment." She obviously turned away and I heard her say "Molly, there's that young man on the phone - Yes! The one you've been talking about all day. (pause) I don't care what position he plays in the rugby team - has he got any money?" There was a scuffling at the other end of the line, then a voice said,

"Hello - is that Frank? Yes it's Molly. Oh I am glad you rang me, I hoped you would!" (We were so unsophisticated it wasn't true!)

I said, "Yes it's me - and if your father would get off me foot I'd like to take you to the pictures on Monday." (The cinemas weren't open on Sundays in those days.)

"Why?" she said.

"Because I think I'm a bit in love with you or summat. Anyway, I'll tell you on Monday if you'll come. Will you?"

"Oh, love," she said. "Of course I will!"

And she did! And I kissed her properly afterwards!

Three nights a week I attended the local tech and at the end of the third term I got a City and Guilds certificate for plumbing. For the practical test I had to take a piece of 4" lead pipe about 3 foot long and ¾" thick, bend it into a right angle (think on it!), with a moleskin wiping cloth, make a metal pot joint to another pipe - no blowlamps were allowed. A lot of skill went into it and I was very pleased with myself. Apart from the 'sustifficate' I got a book on *Modern Plumbing* as a special prize! And I didn't even want to be a plumber! I wanted to paint pictures! What with my scouting, rugby, evening classes and a bit of courting I was pretty busy, but something was missing somehow. I didn't find out until a long while after that around this time Mrs. Steele and my mother had met at a whist drive. The youngsters 'going steady' was discussed and Mr. Steele thought I was a likely lad to go into his business if we 'made a go of it'!

One evening when I arrived home from work Mother met me at the door. "Ee, love," she said. "Come in, I've got something to tell you."

Plonking down a cup of tea on the table, she said, "Listen, you know Uncle Harding died last year? Well, I just got a letter from his solicitors and we've been left three hundred pounds! Ooh, love! We've never been so rich!"

Nancy was sitting at the table with a big smile on her face.

"What about that then, our Mick?"

"Wait a minute, you lot." I hadn't taken it in yet. "Three

hundred pounds! Cor!"

"And Mum wants to rush out and buy one of those new bungalows up on the Moor," said Nancy. "I think she ought to have a holiday first and then we'll think about it. What do you say?"

It was decided there and then! No argument! Mum was to have a holiday! One of Mother's friends with whom she played whist had just returned from two weeks in Bournemouth and she was raving about the place. So, it was decided, Mother should go to Bournemouth and stay with the Yorkshire family for a couple of weeks. When she returned we would discuss our future and that was that!

A couple of weeks later I took her down to the L.M.S. station (London Midland and Scottish for them as don't know wot the initials stand for), settled her in a carriage with a copy of the Yorkshire Post, her luggage, her knitting bag and a lot of etceteras - plus instructions on how to change trains when she got to London. We had three postcards from Bournemouth. She was having a whale of a time - been to four whist drives, an Old-Fashioned Dance at the Pavilion, had a couple of Char-a-bang trips through the New Forest - oh, she had "so much to tell us". Two weeks later I slipped away from work early and met a very sunburned mother at the station. She was bubbling over with excitement - words just tumbled out - "Oo - Frank - the things I've got to tell you both!"

My sister had tea ready when we got home. We sat down and I said, "Now then, Annie Luisa, tell us all about it!"

"Well," she said, "I just can't describe it. It's beautiful! So clean. They don't have tram cars like us, they have trolley buses. You can see the Isle of Wight from there. Oh, the sea is beautiful. The gardens are lovely - they have palm trees and things."

"Give over, Mum - palm trees don't grow in England - it's too cold."

"I tell you, Frank, there are palm trees in the gardens - it's so much warmer down there."

"Well then," I said promptly, "let's go and live there!"

Stunned silence. Mother and Nance gaped at me.

"Live in Bournemouth?" Mother mouthed and looked at Nancy.

"Take no notice, Mother, the lad's daft!" said Nance.

"Wait a minute!" I protested. "Listen, you two. I'm now nineteen and a half, and when I'm twenty-one and done my time I shall be on the dole like everyone else. I might as well be on the dole in Bournemouth as up in Wakefield. With the bit of brass that you have been left we could buy a house down there, or at least put down a deposit." Silence continued - "Nance - could you get a transfer to Bournemouth Telephone Exchange?"

"I've never really thought about it - I expect I could!"

"So, what's to stop us?" I pushed excitedly. "I can get a job of some sort, and I can't get less money than I'm getting now."

"But what about all your friends, love? And Molly? And George? And your rugby?"

The ideas had tumbled out in the space of a few minutes. I hadn't had time to think.

"Well now - there must be a rugger team in Bournemouth. Molly can come down and stay with us every holiday - so can George."

There it was! Resolved. The sea is beautiful — ah!

Now I knew what had been missing in my life in Wakefield. Would I perhaps even own a boat? I was already dragging my family along by their ears but I was sure they would never regret it. I didn't give them much time to think about it either. The following day I handed in my notice - told the boss I would be leaving on Friday.

"Leaving?" he said. "But you're not out of your time yet. Going where? Bournemouth? With a lot of bloody

Southerners? They don't know what plumbing is down there! Why don't you wait a bit and I'll get you a trial with Trinity? You should pack up t'owd Rugby as I've said before and play t'League game and make a bit of brass whilst you're at it. What's wrong with Wakefield anyway? It's a champion little town. Bloody Southerners! You're daft, lad!"

Molly shed a little tear when I broke the news, but I told her about the palm trees and how she would be able to come down on holidays. I promised to write regularly etc. George had applied and been accepted for a job in Andover so he would be leaving the town anyway.

As the train pulled out of Wakefield Station on the Monday morning, little did I think it would be more than twenty years before I saw again the Merrie Cittie. My bike was in the guard's van with my tool-bag lashed to the carrier and I was off to what would be, I thought, a new world. Having five pounds in my pockets it was four pounds nineteen shillings more than Laurie Lee had when he went to Spain - but he did have a fiddle!

Chapter 9

Changing trains in London I trundled my bike along to Waterloo Station. My word, there was more traffic here than there was in Leeds! I was too excited to sit down when I got in the train didn't want to miss anything, so I stood in the corridor whilst I ate the bacon sandwiches Mum had packed for me. After the first half hour the country we were passing through was soft and rolling, it lacked the harshness of Yorkshire or Lancashire. Even the grass seemed to be greener. The train stopped at Southampton, then slowly picking up speed we passed the New Docks. What was that huge liner with the black and red funnels? It must be - it was! The *Queen Mary*. I'd read about it and seen it in the films and had a picture of it in my scrapbook. The New Forest sped by, wild ponies scampering along the railway line. Then Christchurch Harbour with its old Priory sitting at the waters edge came into view. I was bursting with excitement! My digs were with an ex-Yorkshire family who of course made me very welcome.

The following morning I took a trolley bus down to Bournemouth Square. Everything did look cleaner and the people more prosperous than those I had left. Walking through the gardens I saw my first palm trees, the sea, and, there in the distance, the Isle of Wight. You were right ar', Mum, it certainly is a lovely town. Outside the Westover Rowing Club I watched as a crew carried out a long slender craft and deposited it on the beach. Curious, I examined the oars propped up against the wall. Turning to one of the chaps alongside, I said, "These are spoon blades, I know that, but I've never seen looms like these before."

He smiled. "Well, we call them girders because of the cross section - made like that for lightness and strength, of course. Do you do a bit of rowing then?"

"Not really, I've only rowed in a whaler - up North."

"Well, at least you must be able to feather a blade. Do you live down here then?"

"Yes, I've lived here for about twenty hours and I like what I've seen - very much! I'll like it even better when I get a job."

"Why don't you come out with us for a pull? Now," he said, sizing me up. Turning, he said, "Hank - can you lend this bloke some gear?"

"You are coming, aren't you?" he said, grinning.

"But of course - and my name's North, Frank North."

"Bert Spicer," he replied, sticking out his hand. "Welcome to Bournemouth. Hey chaps!" he shouted. "Meet the new boy - Frank North from Yorkshire."

A tall young chap about my own age sauntered up. "I'm Pax Brown, pleased to meet you," he smiled. "Eh, all you tykes play rugger, don't you?"

"Yes," I said, "I played for Wakefield up to about last Saturday. Why?"

"Well, why not come and have a practice game on Tuesday with Bournemouth Rugby Club? What position do you play?"

"Wing forward as a rule."

"Fine - we'll have a beer later and talk about it, eh?"

Well, I'd made about thirty new friends the first day! Not bad for starters! About four days later I got a job digging drains for a new hotel. The name of my new employers was Mumford, Bailey and Preston, known locally as Mumble, Bumble and Effing Grumble. However, as I was to be paid two pounds ten shillings a week I couldn't have cared less!

My mother and sister followed me down a few weeks later when Nancy's transfer came through to Boscombe Telephone Exchange. Just like that! A deposit went down quickly on a pretty little bungalow near Hengistbury Head with glorious views of Christchurch Harbour, the Isle of Wight, and the sea. I made a garden with a rockery, lawn, fishpond, and rose trees. Never had I seen my mother so happy. She'd walk for miles picking up horse-droppings with a bucket and shovel for those rose trees. My sister and I both had jobs and it was the first time for many years that we didn't have to share our house with lodgers.

Most evenings I went down to the Rowing Club. I had a regular position at No. 3 in the junior crew. Unlike the inland boatclubs the 'Fours' were built heavier and stronger, as they were used on the open sea and in rough water, so, although we concentrated on style, brawn was very necessary. So much so, the following season we took our wider blades to Oxford, winning the Senior, Junior and Maiden Fours at the Civic Regatta in 1937. Howzat! During that winter, I played wing forward for Bournemouth Club in their First Fifteen.

The job I was doing was very hard physically, which I didn't mind, it was first class training, but the foreman was a right bastard, a real Cor-Blimey-Cockney - and an authority on every bloody thing! He sneered at everyone who hadn't been fortunate enough to be born in the Smoke within sound of Bow bells. The foreman was Chairman of the local Plumbers' Union too. He put me against Socialism more than anyone I had ever met. Joining the Union of course was obligatory, but when he gave a sneering "Fraternal greetings to Brother North from Yorkshire who has come South to learn the trade as it should be done," I thought, "Up you, mate!" I paid my weekly subs and never again in my life went to another union meeting.

Every evening when I had finished work, I stole a couple

of rustic bricks, and in a couple of weeks had sufficient to make a sundial for the garden, the face itself I cut out of heavy lead sheet. For a couple of weeks I had been feeling groggy. Three times a day I had to go to the heads, much to the disgust of Cockney Gaffer who accused me of malingering. I had a rotten headache all that day, and cycling home in the evening I passed out and fell off my bike. Eventually Mother insisted that I go to bed, and sent for the doctor who came promptly, and said at once, "Typhoid fever." Unknown yet to the general public, there was a typhoid epidemic raging in Bournemouth. Would you believe? This news had been kept quiet. The City Fathers, with an eye on tourism, had clamped down on all news coverage. It was many years after that I learned that the fever outbreak was found to be caused by contaminated milk from the town's biggest dairy.

An emergency hospital had been opened in Hadden Hall Woods just outside the town, where I was incarcerated for six weeks, only to find, when I was eventually discharged, that my job had been given to another man and I was on the dole with thousands of other young men. Sod it! I scoured the building sites looking for any job going, but to no avail. In the evenings I made 'genooine' model galleons which I sold for one guinea each. It helped, but after two or three weeks I was getting discouraged at not finding a job.

One evening after supper, Nancy said, "'Ere, our Mick, what about enquiring at the Post Office Engineering Department? I've heard the chaps talking and there is a big new exchange being built at Bournemouth and they have been taking on some new men."

"But I know nothing about electricity, Nancy, and there must be thousands of chaps to pick from."

"Well, at least you could go down to the Telephone House and see," said Big Sister. "Tomorrow."

The following day I cycled down to Bournemouth taking

with me various working drawings I had done at the tech in Wakefield. I was shown into the office of a Mr. Blewdon, the Chief Engineer. He was very sympathetic, but said of course plumbing certificates weren't going to help much in a telephone exchange.

"Er," he stopped and thought for a moment. "Mr. North, I don't suppose you have any knowledge of sign-writing, have you?"

Oh, I'm quick - sharp as a razor! "Sign-writing, Mr. Blewdon? As a matter of fact I did quite a bit when I was up North." (Gawd forgive me!)

"Really? That's very interesting - very interesting! Bring me some samples of your work on Friday morning - at about this time. I've got an idea!"

I'd never written a sign in my life, but I had always been keen on drawing and painting - it couldn't be so hard, could it? On my way home I stopped at Boscombe Arcade, went into the art shop and bought a sixpenny copy of *Simple Lettering and How to do it*. For the next couple of days I practised lettering, rubbing it out and doing it again. On Friday morning I took my piece of plywood covered with letters and numbers, all in glorious technicolor, down to Telephone House.

"My word," said the Chief Engineer when I was shown into his office, "this is very good. I'm most impressed - not that I know anything about this sort of thing - but it is just what we are looking for! How long did it take you to do this, Mr. North?"

"Oh," I said airily, "an hour, an hour and a half maybe."

"I'm going to keep this sample of your work. Start at the New Exchange in Bournemouth on Monday morning at eight o'clock, and in the meantime I'll have a word with the engineer in charge. Nice to have met you Mr. North and the best of luck!"

When I got home I put my bike against the wall as Mum

opened the door. "How did you get on, lad?" she said rather anxiously.

"Start at the New Exchange on Monday morning at eight o'clock. Annie, me dear, you are talking to a Post Office Engineer! How about that!"

She gave me a rather wobbly smile and a big tear ran down her cheek. "Ooh, lad!" she said, "a government job. You're settled for life! You'll never be out of work again." Bless her old heart!

Monday morning - I wasn't late this time - I reported to the engineer in charge - Charlie (Banger) Keefe, who showed me where my lettering was required. It was very simple work and, as Mr. Blewdon said, he didn't know much about it, and Charlie obligingly said - he didn't either - and, as I had read the sixpenny book, I felt quite knowledgeable! Being the only sign-writer in the area I found that I was much in demand. I learned much about the lovely counties of Hampshire and Dorset being chauffeured around in the little Post Office vans to do my daily stint. The P.O. regulations stated that thirty-two digits per hour should be produced, assuming digits included stops and commas I reckoned to suffer about four hours work daily. The remainder of the time I spent sketching, painting and visiting boatyards. It was much better than digging trenches for drains.

August and September were the months in which all the South Coast Regattas were held, and the Wet-Bobs trained to be at their peak at this time of year. Most Saturdays the Boat Club spent travelling to Southampton - Weymouth, Poole etc. with the 'galleys' to compete in the rowing events. One of the club members provided us with a big wagon which we fitted out with removable racks to hold three boats; the oars were lashed inside and the crews piled on board clad in gorgeous red, black, and white striped blazers - guaranteed to slay any girls in sight. Win or lose, we always stopped at our favourite pub on the way back home, making a general nuisance of ourselves, drinking too much beer, and singing dirty rugby songs at the tops of our voices. For instance - do any oldies remember *Mobile*?

> *There's a shortage of good bogs in Mobile*
> *There's a dearth of good toilets in Mobile*
> *There's a shortage of good bogs*
> *So we wait until it clogs*
> *Then we saw it off in logs in Mobile.*

Aside: "You can't write that," said my Missus, "it's mucky."
"But it's History, girl, it's History!"

Later during the rugby season I was very proud to be picked to play wing forward for the county, and got an awful thumping in the first game I played - against Cornwall - I was concussed for the latter part of the game and didn't come around until well after the game was over. I was pushed under a cold shower and congratulated for scoring a try! I didn't remember a thing about it!

Anyone who is stupid enough to play rugby can expect to get hurt. That's the sort of silly game it is, but nobody hurts another chap deliberately. There was one big joker who played for Weymouth - however, he was about sixteen stone and a right dirty sod. Taff Jones was about thirty-six years old, past his prime, but he had forgotten more about rugger than I remember. He was our pack leader.

"Right, boys," he said. "We'll settle his hash."

"Next time we get the ball, whoever gets it kick it up in the air so Fatso catches it! Then I want eight forwards on top of him." Behind the scrum the next time we got the ball, the stand-off belted it up in the air. There was King Kong waiting for it. Eight forwards hit him all at once and we left him stuck in the mud like a starfish. Three times that happened, and the fourth time, instead of running to catch it, he stopped to tie his shoelace! We never had any more agro from him! Ever!

"North," said Taffy one afternoon, "this is a heavy pack we're up against. Please don't break off on your own and go frigging off with the three-quarters. 'Cos if you do, you'll get my boot up your arse!" He was past his prime, but he was built like a Sherman tank. So I didn't! Good old Taff. (He died at Alamein. Alas!)

Unfortunately, later that season I was tackled by two blokes at the same time - one of them grabbed my right ankle whilst his mate crashed into my knee, tearing the cartilage and stretching the tendons. I rolled on the ground - swore loudly and said "Bollocks!" A young student doctor playing for the opposite side - a very keen type - promptly pulled down my shorts and started massaging the wrong part of my anatomy with Sloan's Liniment. It was very painful and certainly not the way to treat the family jewels! One of the chaps ran me home in his car and I was put to bed for ten days until the fluid in my knee disappeared. Still classed as 'Temporary' at the G.P.O., I received no pay whilst off work, so I strapped up my leg and had a walking stick with which to hobble around.

A workmate living nearby took me to and from work on his motorbike, which was all very well until one day he took the corner of a gate too closely and my leg, sticking out sideways, hit the gatepost. Ouch! For years afterwards I had to wear an elastic knee bandage, and although I did try to play rugby again, my leg always packed up on me, giving me a lot of pain and building up fluid which of course meant rest and time off work - which I couldn't afford. Apparently the standard cartilage operation wouldn't suffice because of the stretched tendons - there was no remedy for that in those days.

Molly had been coming down to stay with us for the holidays, but our letters had become few and far between. There was a sure lessening of interest on both sides. George, over for the weekend from Andover with the latest from

Wakefield, told me Molly had suddenly got engaged to an old fellow called Atkinson - he must have been all of thirty years of age!

I still kept up my rowing, until the following September when I had a disagreement with the Racing Committee. The finals for the South Coast Championship were to be rowed off between Westover R.C. and Southampton Coal Porters. We had two boats in the race, and the strategy was that our 'B' crew should "accidentally" ram Coaty's whilst 'A' crew pulled for the finish. I stood up and strongly objected to this, saying that I was rowing for fun and ramming another boat just wasn't on! On being told by the Club Captain that this was the most prestigious race of the season, I retorted that, that being the case, they had better get another No. 3 man. So they did - and I never rowed seriously again. I still used the club however and remained good friends with everyone. So! What did I do then? No rugby, no rowing and no courting! I bought a boat!

She was lying in the mud of Tuckton Creek on the River Stour at Christchurch, half a mile from my home, was full of water and looked very decrepit. Thirty feet long with a very shallow draft, a big iron centre board, a large open cockpit, funny rounded cabin-top and a forty-eight foot mast with diamond rigging - she was obviously an old Broads boat. Along with a ten-foot dinghy, I bought her for nine pounds! It was all the money I had - but to hell with the expense! I had my own boat at last! The local old sweats said that I'd never keep her tight. Nearly drowned a couple of chaps, she had! Wouldn't answer the helm! Don't touch her with a bargepole! She had a lovely set of cotton sails made by Ratsey's and Lapthorne. I burned off and painted the dinghy. It looked pretty good too, but when I was offered ten pounds for it I nearly snatched the man's hand off! Anyway, I couldn't afford a dinghy and a yacht. Having cut ten feet off her mast, I then scraped and varnished it. I shortened all the stanchions and rigging, soaked the rigging screws in oil and paraffin and spliced them on. She began to look like a boat again. But I couldn't get her tight! She leaked like a basket. I dried her out and carefully caulked the garboards, but I did it from the inside - not knowing any better - and she still leaked - naturally! Creeping down at night I pumped her out again when no one was about. One very cold night whilst doing this I slipped on the ice-covered deck and fell in the 'oggin. Unfortunately I had plus-fours on, which promptly filled with icy water, and I had to hang on to the boat's counter for ten minutes, gradually creeping up over the stern until they had drained out. It's a tough life at sea! I sailed t'old boat up and down Christchurch Harbour for the remainder of that season, not daring to take her outside, learning a lot and developing fantastic pumping muscles. One September afternoon a rather natty gentleman, dressed in a blazer and grey slacks, asked if I would sell the boat. I said, "Yes, but not for less than twenty pounds."

"Fifteen," said the man, "if I can sail her to Holland."

"Fifteen it is," I said. "And you can take her wherever you want." Well he could, couldn't he? "There's money in shipping," I thought, collected his fifteen pounds in my hot little hand and wished him the best of British luck!

A few days later, whilst working in Weymouth, having done my stint of thirty-two digits per hour, wandering along the quayside, I sauntered into a small boatyard near the lifeboat station.

"Can I help you, young feller?" said a voice.

"Well, I want a boat," I said, "but I only have fifteen pounds."

"That's not very much," said the owner of the yard, coming out of an old boatshed, "I doubt if you'll get a 'J' class cutter for that sort of brass." He started to fill his pipe, then stopped. Poking the cherry-wood into my chest, he said, "Eh - wait a minute. Give us a hand!" Walking back into the shed he started shifting spars, old rudders and lifejackets, and, under a pile of dusty sails, a clinker-built bow came to light.

"This is one of the old Lea-on-Solent 'one designs,'" he said. "Must've been 'ere nigh on ten years. Wait a minute and I'll get a torch and you can look inside of 'e."

It was seventeen feet long, nice and beamy, had a big galvanised centre-board and rather a lot of 'tumble-home' for such a small boat. "Good little sea boat," I thought, remembering Uffa Fox's words of wisdom. "Is there any gear with her, Skipper?"

"She has some sails of sorts, if I remember rightly - be in one o' those lockers I reckon. There's a roller reefing boom and a sort of roller spar headsail. 'E mast is split - it's up there on that spar rack, but 'appen it could be spliced or summat."

"What do you want for t'owd boat then?" I queried, having already mentally put a small cabin-top on it, and a couple of small bunks below deck.

"Well now, I reckon I could let 'e go for thirty quid," he said.

"But I've only got fifteen! Honestly! I could mebbe borrow five pounds from my mother, but I know she wouldn't be able to lend me any more."

"But that's only twenty pounds," he said.

"Right, I'll have it," said Shylock North. "Here's my fifteen pounds, and I'll bring the other five pounds on Saturday when I come to collect the boat." I left the yard in a hazy glow and the boatyard owner with his head on one side, scratching his bald spot with the end of his cherry-wood pipe.

Come Saturday my crew and I turned up at the boatyard as promised. Ron Williams had come to give me a hand to sail it around to Christchurch - about fifty miles down the coast. Willie played fullback for Bournemouth Rugby Club, pulled a very good No. 2 oar for Westover, but had never before done any sailing. Earlier in the week I had left a message for the yard to get the mast down to splice it and put three copper straps around it, then put her in the water and let her plim up. After so many years in a shed the hull was dry as a bone and sure enough it had leaked like a sieve. But, being built of spruce, she'd tightened up nicely, and when we sponged it out it didn't leak a drop. After paying my dues to the owner of the yard we put a crate of beer on board and a large cherry cake. I explained port and starboard to Willie, we hoisted the old brown mainsail, pulled the headsail out of its wooden roller (I'd never seen one of these gadgets before) and away we went, turning to port at the harbour entrance.

I didn't have a compass or a chart but reckoned from the A.A. map it must be about easterly - sort of. *Half-Pint* was running briskly downwind. (Her previous name - half obliterated on the stern was *Gill*, and to any drinking man from North of the Trent, a gill was $1/2$ a pint.) Willie was slurping happily at a bottle of Huntsman's Ale, and I no doubt was grinning from ear to ear. I had a boat and it didn't leak! What about that! This euphoric state of affairs however didn't last long - offshore the wind increased rapidly and lumps of rock kept appearing when I wasn't expecting them, and I had to stand out farther to seaward. Willie was sea-sick. I really should have taken in a reef but I didn't dare leave the helm.

According to my map, St. Albans should be the next headland. The old boat was going like a train, the waves were getting higher, steeper and sliding back on themselves. Overfalls? St. Albans Race? I must have read about it somewhere. Was there an inside passage? I think (- I hope!). We crept closer inshore. Bloody great rocks kept creeping up on us. The cliffs got higher and higher, seemingly going on forever. The mast gave a couple of short, sharp wiggles and fell over on the side! The old sod at the boatyard had got his own back. Instead of strapping the long break in the mast, he'd driven in three iron nails and covered them with tape, bloody old monkey! Mast, sails and rigging wrapped themselves around the boat. We broached to and every second wave flopped into the cockpit. Willie couldn't care less! Bottles of Huntsman's Ale were swimming about and, I remember thinking that all those floating cherries couldn't have come from one cake. Grabbing a bucket, I started to bail with one hand - the other was on the tiller, and tentatively suggested to my crew that perhaps, if it wasn't too much to ask, he'd get off his bloody arse and start pumping, being as we had now only nine inches free board and no life-jackets.

Bucketing and pumping we managed to keep half afloat, when lo! - about an hour later a great big white cabin cruiser came into view astern of us. As she came alongside she looked as big as a row of houses. A smartly dressed hand threw me a rope - about as fat as my leg - which I turned up around the stump of the mast. Snatching up armfuls of wet sails, rigging and various spars, I piled them on top of a very supine, wet Willie, grabbed the tiller and nearly flopped over the transom as the big yacht went ahead at X number of knots, and we went steaming down the south coast of England - up to my thighs in water as the boat lifted. Willie said, "Shit!" and puked again, whilst the nattily dressed owner - our Saviour, sat an his bum on his after-deck taking movies of the whole perishin' shambles. We were towed eventually into Poole, the owner dropping us off the Parkstone Yacht Club to the great amusement of the local ladies. I have before me a cutting from the Bournemouth Chronicle of that date:

Headlines: Sailing boat minus mast. Swanage Lifeboat called out, exciting visitors.

They were excited? What about Willie and me!

Chapter 10

In September of that year war was declared. Germany had invaded Poland, Mr. Chamberlain told us on the radio whilst I was sitting at anchor off Mudeford. That first week I applied to join the Royal Navy but was told that I was in a reserved occupation. A million telephones were needed in thousands of service camps "Thanks for the offer. We'll keep you informed." The year of the Phoney War went by - all my friends were joining the armed services. Willie was in the R.A.F., serving as a Sergeant Pilot, and Paxie Brown went into the Royal Navy. Bert Spicer, always a car fanatic, had just bought a bull-nosed Morris for ten pounds and he loved it to death. He naturally joined the R.A.S.C. He was commissioned in that regiment, and with visions of commanding a squadron of armoured cars, ended up on the north-west frontier of India in charge of one hundred and twenty mules! Just another square peg. And where was I? Painting G.P.O. on thousands of tin hats! George went into the Royal Engineers, managed to scramble back from Dunkirk and was commissioned three months later. I tried the Merchant Navy.

"Sorry, old man - love to have you but you're reserved."

More tin hats. Even the telephone operators had them tucked under their chairs. The lining of the British steel helmet was fastened to the top with a big, flattish, round-headed screw. Remember? Sitting bored as hell one day, I picked up my own helmet and on it painted a luscious blonde, looking over her shoulder, lifting up her skirt waist high and showing her bottom (the slot in the screw) with a little caption underneath saying, "Ass'oles to Adolf" - very patriotic!

"Blimey, Franky," said Banger Keefe, " paint me one like that!"

Alfie Faithfull, my inspector - he saw it.

"Bl-bl-bloody 'ell, F-F-Franky - you'd better p-p-paint me one as well - and d-d-don't p-put it on your t-t-timesheet either!"

The Area Engineer sent me a memo: "One for me and one for the Chief Clerk - pronto!"

What had I done?

I had to do all the bloody tin hats again - this time in technicolor! It got to the stage where I charged a pint of ale in the canteen for one of them. I could have been drunk for twenty-four hours a day. What a way to fight the Germans! What with Jane undressing in the Daily Mirror and my painting of 'Beautiful Bums' I reckon we did more to boost morale than the new Prime Minister, Winston Churchill. Then came the order "All G.P.O. personnel will join the L.D.V." (What's that, Grandad? Local Defence Volunteers, lad - where's your knowledge of modern warfare?) This, of course, later became the Home Guard, a much superior regiment, as we then changed our arm-bands to proper khaki uniforms and a funny 'at, you didn't wear it, you walked alongside it. We were issued with Ross rifles (Boer War vintage) and a clip of five cartridges. There were eventually so many bullet-holes in the ceiling of Telephone House, however, that we had to hand in the cartridges and to stand guard on the roof with fixed bayonets. ("When I say 'Fix' - you don't fix, when I say 'bayonets' you whips 'em out and whops 'em on! Right?" "Right Sergeant.")

Due to this change in wartime strategy, we all given instruction on how to impale a falling German paratrooper on the roof of Telephone House with a bayonet. Cross my heart and hope to die if that's not the truth! And Napoleon had the French sauce to say that the British were a nation of shopkeepers. Then some clot in Head Office said "As 'ow Mr. North is an Engineer? Yes?"

"Of course."

"Can he fit a telephone?"

"Who? Franky? Give over! He doesn't know an ohm from a hole in the ground."

"This should be rectified - there's a war on, y'know!"

"So I've heard. So what?"

"Send him on a course, that's what."

"Who's going to do the sign-writing?"

"Get a girl to do it from the art college or, er, somewhere."

The upshot was that I was given a railway warrant, a big fat loose-leaf book on *How to fit a telephone in three easy lessons* and sent away to Avonmouth (Where's that Grandad? Shut up, twit!) to become qualified, knowing full well that if and when I should be called up I would be drafted into the Royal Corps of Signals like the remainder of the Post Office engineers. What a way to run a war. What a waste of shining talent - me a Brown type! I went to Avonmouth. At the end of the course I was shaken by the hand and was told that as a pass was 45 marks and I had achieved 45½ (you'd never believe!) - I was qualified to join the club, I arsk you!

Back at Bournemouth I was issued with a kit of tools, another book of unreadable diagrams and told to get fitting. Mounting my bicycle, I fastened my shiny new toolbag onto the handlebars, cuddling a telephone (candlestick type, Mark 2). I trundled away to No. 11 Wellington Road. I do not tell a lie! This is a fact! Parking my bike, I walked up the drive and rang the doorbell. The door opened immediately.

"Good morning, madam," I said, "G.P.O. - I've come to fit your telephone."

"How nice, do come in, young man - I was just going shopping, as you can see," and she gestured to the hat she was wearing and the outdoor coat.

"Oh, in that case, I'll come around tomorrow," I said, quick as a flash.

"No, no, I wouldn't hear of it," and she toddled back down the passage.

Sod it!

The whole inside of the house was painted white, the doors, surrounds and picture-rails beautifully enamelled.

"You do have white covered wire, of course?"

"Of course, m'am, and white staples."

"I'm so glad. As you can see, the room has only just been decorated. Now then, I want the phone on that table. I shan't be long, then perhaps we could have a cup of tea. 'Bye for now." She tripped out of the room and the front door clicked shut.

Looking around I saw that a small connecting box had been fastened to the window frame, along the picture rail, down the side of the door, and along the skirting board (which was about twelve inches deep with four rounded mouldings along the top). Picking up my hammer and popping a handful of staples into my mouth I bent down and banged in the first one, being very careful not to mark the paint. Up the window frame, along the picture rail and down the side of the door. Not a mark anywhere! Proper job! Fitting telephones? Money for old rope! Bending the wire along the top skirting-board, I pressed in the points of the next staple and gave it a sharp clout with the hammer. Bang! Flash!

I fell over backwards spitting staples all over the carpet. There were long black streaks burned into the paint and a nasty brown scorch-mark along the top of the skirting. What I had assessed as a long moulding on the top of the wood was a thick electric cable covered with coats of white enamel. Kee-rist! Pulling out the staple with a pair of insulated pliers, and chopping the wire down to the next moulding, I slapped in staples like clockwork. Cutting off the wire to length, I stripped it, connected it to the instrument, said a short, sharp prayer, and rang exchange.

"Number please," said a lovely female voice.

"Engineer here, miss - will you ring me back on this number please."

Bur-up! Bur-up! Bur-up!

"Thank you, miss, sorry you've been troubled," and put down the earpiece.

Scrambling my tools together, I paused at the door on the way out and flipped on a couple of light-switches. Nothing! Nada! O shit! Opening the door I bumped into the lady-owner as she was about to put the key in the lock.

"My word, young man, you've been quick! Finished already? I was just going to make a cup of tea."

"Very kind of you, madam, but we have so much work on these days. There's a war on, you know, ha ha!"

Down the drive, onto my bike and way down Wellington Road. Whether the poor lady had any lights in her house for the remainder of the war I don't know, but I felt that somehow this wasn't my vocation either!

Some of the chaps in the department were now filtering into the army (Signals Corps, of course), but I was sent to Andover to assist in the enlarging of the old Telephone Exchange.

"Have you got any digs, Franky?" I was asked by my chum.

"No, I've only just got off the bus, Nev."

"It's a hell of a job getting lodgings these days," he said, "Salisbury Plain is crawling with squaddies trying to get accommodation for their wives, but wait a minute, perhaps my landlady would make you up a camp-bed in my room. There is no hot water and only an outside loo, but she's a good soul, let's ask her."

All this was arranged satisfactorily, and that evening Neville Saunders and I went out and had a few beers. He also was a member of the Westover Rowing Club and he liked his beer too. We arrived back at our lodgings in the black-out, very happy and well after closing time. It was a very still night. We opened the door as quietly as we could, making exaggerated "shushing" noises as we tripped over the brass stair rods. As we got into the bedroom, Nev said, "Blimey, Northy, I couldn't 'arf do with a pee."

"So could I, mate, but we can't go downstairs again in the dark - we shall wake up the whole flipping house."

"Eh, let's open the window and we can tiddle on the flowerbed."

"Good idea!"

The window hadn't been opened for years, but with a few squeaks we managed to slide up the lower sash.

"Oo, I'm bursting," said Nev. "Ready?"

"Not 'arf!"

We both took a deep breath and thankfully let go - fifteen feet down on a corrugated iron roof!

"Wassat, Fred?" came a voice from the next bedroom, "I didn't 'ear no air-raid warning."

A warden in pyjamas and a tin hat scuttled across the darkened street with a bucketful of water and a hand pump.

"Incendiaries," he was waffling.

We couldn't stop, but we reduced the noise slightly by peeing against the rain-water pipes. I tell you - war is hell!

Chapter 11

Back in Bournemouth some weeks later, I received a telephone call. On answering, a feminine voice with a slight Aussie accent said, "Hello, remember me? Irene."

"But of course," I said, thinking fast. "How are you getting on?" I remembered meeting her at a party a couple of weeks previously. She was slim and blonde with a lovely figure, and we had danced together and laughed a lot. "As a matter of fact," I said gallantly, "I wanted to ring you but didn't remember your second name." (Fast thinking, North!)

"Well now, isn't that nice," she said, "I thought you might think me rather naughty phoning you like this, but I'm invited to a rather special party and my partner has been called back to his regiment. I thought you were rather nice, and I wondered if you would help me out? Mother has lent me the Lanchester and we are all right for petrol. I could run you home afterwards. Will you come?"

"But of course, I should be delighted."

I escorted her to the party and it was very nice too. She ran me home afterwards, we had a cuddle in the car and I arranged to meet her the following evening.

Her family owned one of the biggest and most prestigious hotels in town. They were very rich. Her parents had divorced when she was a little girl, her father emigrating to Western Australia taking Irene with him. Later, her mother married the very wealthy owner of the hotel, and, with his demise some years later, became majority shareholder and Managing Director. She sent to Aussie for her daughter, insisted that she have elocution lessons, had her taught tennis and dancing by professionals, gave her a nice allowance, and turned her loose. Good on 'er! Beaut! Being invited by her to cocktails and dinner parties, I was introduced to all the relatives.

"Frank is in the Civil Service or something, (Well, I was, wasn't I?) Must be rather hush-hush. He's dying to get into the Navy, but can't join up yet - y'know - reserved."

With my issue blue Post Office mac over my dinner jacket, I would cycle down to the hotel, take off my cycle clips, hide my bike in the bushes, run a comb through my hair and saunter in through the front door, winking at the hall porter who would give me a grave smile and say, "Good evening, Mr. North." The first time he said it I looked around for my father - and he'd been dead for fifteen years. Everybody else called me Franky or Northy. Irene wore the most beautiful clothes and toted me around in this big brown car. I thought she was smashing!

She was related to the Foxes of Glacier Mint fame and had done a bit of yachting with them. They had a cruiser with a tennis court on deck, and when I told her about *Half-Pint* she said she loved boats and could she see it. "It's not very big," I said, but she was all agog and arranged to come down to Tuckton on Saturday afternoon. I was helping the gang shore up a big fishing boat when the car turned the corner into Jim Newlyn's boatyard. The chauffeur in the brown livery hopped out and opened the door for her. Irene stepped out, waved and walked down the lane, the driver following with a big picnic hamper held up to his chest.

"Hello," she said, "hello, everybody." She smiled and I introduced her to the chaps. She was very brown and wore a very lovely low cut silk dress and white high-heeled sandals.

"Cor! Blimey," whispered young Charlie, "what a smasher!"

We walked down to *Half-Pint* lying alongside the jetty.

"What a dear little boat," she said as I helped her on board. Kicking off her shoes she crawled into the cabin where I had been painting the deckhead.

"Oo, I like painting," she said, "can I finish it off for you?"

"But, of course," said I, "you can't paint in that outfit though, you'd better put on this old shirt of mine."

"Good-o! Wait a tick." She slipped out of her dress and I got a glimpse of frothy little white panties and the tiny bra she was very nearly wearing - as she slipped my shirt over her head. "Can I use this?" It was a very old Rugby Club scarf.

"Certainly," I said, so she tied up her long blonde hair into a coil and wrapped the scarf around it.

"Northy!" came a shout from up the lane. "Give us a hand with these shores - won't take a minute."

"Must go and help them," I apologized. "They're holding up about three and a half tons of fishing boat."

"That's okay - leave me here - I shall be quite happy."

"Sure?"

"I'll call when I need another drum of paint."

Three quarters of an hour later I washed the mud off my hands and ambled down to *Half-Pint*. Irene was lying in a pool of white paint and as she slapped it on the deck-head it was running down her arm and dripping off her elbow.

She beamed. "Like it? - Doesn't it make the cabin look much bigger?"

"Well - er - it certainly looks different," I said, gazing at her long, brown legs. "Never seen the inside of a boat look so nice. Anyway, shall I make a cuppa?" .

"Smithers brought a couple of flasks of tea with the sandwiches in the hamper - shall I go down and get it?"

"Not like that, m'dear," I said, thinking of the boys on the jetty, "I'll get it."

And very nice too. Fresh salmon sandwiches and little

biscuits with caviar stuck on top, a fruit cake big enough to choke a horse and a flask of tea each.

"That's my girl," I thought - and I can teach her to paint as we go along.

We were married not long after this. Irene's love for boats did not last. To begin with we were happy. Our son, Michael, was born in 1941. But, like many other wartime marriages, ours did not make the grade. We remained good friends. Michael lived with my mother and sister.

Chapter 12

One afternoon I was reading an article in a newspaper about a gang of Bogside Irish - calling themselves the I.R.A. They were putting bombs into letter-boxes and knocking bobbies' helmets off. Trying to free the Auld Country from the British yoke. Holy Mary! Mother of God! Tis idjuts they are - they are! I should have been sign-writing - but it was too late to start now - 5:45! Fiddling around, bored to tears, I found a piece of blue chalk on a shelf. With nothing else to do, I wrote on the battery-room door: "Beware! The I.R.A. have found you out!"

Someone upstairs shouted, "Franky, do you want a lift home? I'm going your way!"

I scampered off upstairs, grabbing my coat as I went.

The following morning, I parked my bike and was just walking through the door of the exchange when I was grabbed on each arm by a big policeman. "What's going on? J—"

"Shut up! In here!"

I was bundled into the adjoining room where Alfie Faithfull stood with the chief engineer and a police inspector.

"Who is this man?" said the inspector, looking at me very fiercely.

"Franky N-n-n-n-orth," said Alfie.

"What religion are you?"

"C. of E."

Turning to Alfie he said, "Could you vouch for this person?"

"A-a-a-s m-m-m-much as anybody," said Alfie with a grin.

"This isn't funny, Mr. Faithfull," said the Law and, turning to me, said - "I.D. card!"

This I gave him with my P.O. Pass.

He looked at it. "Right - release him. Next!"

Old Brummy was hauled in, looking very scared.

"What's going on then?" I said as I was hanging up my coat.

"They ain't saying, but I think it's an I.R.A. scare," said someone. "Blimey, if they blow this joint up we'll have all those bloody cables to lay again!"

"Funny," I thought, "I was only reading about those bastards last night. Fancy those twits coming to Bournemouth!"

Chapter 13

My call-up papers came through at last! Report at *H.M.S. Collingwood*, Fareham, Hants at 11:30 hours Monday, October 2nd, 1942. Chop chop! Hoorah! Good old Chiefy! *H.M.S. Collingwood* was the training establishment for new entries Portsmouth Division, Royal Navy. I stood outside the gates, suitcase in hand, civil gas-mask at the ready. Peering over the wall, I counted about fifty heads on t'other side, some in flat caps, others in bowler hats, some in knitted titfers. Well, this is what it's all about, Northy - get in! I walked through the gates, puffing at my pipe to give me confidence.

" - And you can put that bloody pipe out, Jack! Right quick!" bellowed a stentorian voice in my ear, and a petty officer in white belt and gaiters pushed past me, shouting profanities at all and sundry. "Get fell in, you 'effing lot!" he barked. "In threes by yonder door! Now!"

The miscellaneous collection of would-be sailors surged forward, tripping over their conglomeration of bags, suitcases, rucksacks and paper parcels. We were counted, recounted, pushed into line, vaccinated, inoculated, counted again, fell in, then marched off in threes to our new home - a Nissen Hut - by one of a group of C.P.O.'s, who were to be our instructors for the next three months. My hut, No. 34, was under the watchful eye of C.P.O. Glasspole, a Naval Reservist, called up for the duration. He was known from that day forward as Bulldog. The following morning we breakfasted on porridge, then bacon and bangers floating around in tinned tomato sauce - known as Red Lead. "Gawd," I muttered, "I can't eat this mess!"

"Can't you, mate? Well, I can," and a pair of hands shipped away my plate before I could have second thoughts. Then we were square-bashing.

"You, Lofty," said the chief, pointing to me. "Take charge 'ere! March these buggers around whilst I have a pee!"

This I did, feeling very pleased with myself. Remembering the drill from the Home Guard I turned them about, double-timed them and was getting along splendidly until the leading file were marched into a brick wall. I had forgotten the command to halt. "'Whoa'!" I yelled as they were marking time with their noses up against the brickwork.

"'Whoa'?" roared a voice behind me. "'Whoa'? They're not bleedin' 'orses! You're not in the 'effing cavalry!"

"Please don't say 'whoa'," the instructor whispered. "Just say ''alt' and they'll 'alt. Just you see."

"Now," he roared. "Get fell in again!"

But I saw at once how power could go to one's head - having had a taste of it!

On our first morning, after breakfast we were all fell in and marched down to the 'slops' to be kitted out. Two petty officers threw our gear at us. Hats, jumpers, lanyards, trousers, two of each - one for best and one for going ashore, two pairs of boots, a seaman's manual, knife with marine spike, brown cardboard ditty box, knife, fork and spoon, and a kit bag in which to stow them. Two woollen vests, long underpants, three pairs of navy socks and two collars, a pair of gym shoes, gas-mask, overcoat etc. etc. Whether these clothes fitted or not didn't really matter to the supply ratings, so after we were marched back to our hut there was a big shmozzle as we swapped them all with our new mates until eventually we all got articles that fitted us (more or less). Mind you, no matlo, if he wanted to look 'tiddly' (smart) would go ashore dressed in 'pusser' rig. The collars each had a hole punched in the lining, then they were put under a running hot water tap to bleach and give them 'sea-time'. The hat ribbon with the tally 'H.M.S.' was taken off and given to an old sweat who, for two shillings and sixpence, would make a sixteen point bow to sit over the left eye with the tanner in the centre. Very important! The black silk (evidently we were still in mourning for the death of Nelson) was carefully folded and laid between the pages of the seaman's manual. After one day's wear all white underclothing was stained navy blue and had to be washed daily - it took at least a month to get them white and all of us had dark blue ankles until the blue dye from the socks had washed out.

After about one week we were allowed 'ashore' (out of the gate) and everyone boarded the bus for Portsmouth, where all would-be-tiddly sailors bought navy caps with a red and green, port and starboard, lining. Some even went to the expense of buying new suits cut so tight that their mates had to help get them off and on, and many came back on board with tattoos, just to prove what deep-sea men they were.

As I was the oldest inhabitant I was made Hut Leader, and, due to my great age, twenty-four, was known as Uncle or, usually, Nonkey. Most of the chaps were in their late teens and I got great satisfaction from beating them at gym and being the first 'up an' over' the rigging which was held up by two huge sailing ship masts on the parade ground. After three days we were allowed to join in 'Divisions'. We stood to attention as the White Ensign was hoisted to the strains of the Band of the Royal Marines. A big tear trickled down my cheek - silly old me, but I was so proud to be in the Royal Navy at last.

After three weeks' training we all had to visit the psychologist to be informed as to which branch of the service we were best suited. When my turn came I entered the office and stood to attention.

"Relax," said the rather bored looking gentleman sitting at his desk. "Stand easy - I'm not Navy, you know, I'm a civilian. Sit down if you wish. Now then," he murmured, "let's see - er - oh yes, we have examined your paper carefully and decided that you will serve your country best as a - pause - motor mechanic." He looked up and gave me a weary smile, as though doing me a great favour.

"Well, that's rather stupid," I said, "I can't even drive a car." (I didn't learn until I was forty).

"Well, North - that's what it is to be according to your paper."

"What paper?" I queried.

"The one you filled in when you joined."

I grinned. "Oh, you can forget about that," I said despairingly.

"Why, weren't you feeling very well?"

"I never felt better, but I was in a hell of a hurry." And I explained the circumstances.

"Well, old man," he said smugly, "you only get one paper."

"Why, haven't you got any more of them?"

He scowled. "I've got a bagful here - but you only get one chance."

"Mate," I said, leaning over the desk and looking him in the eye. "Who is going to fight the bloody Germans? Me or you? Give me another paper, it's no skin off your nose."

He was, as he had said, a civilian and not a Naval Officer or I shouldn't have taken the chance. I got my paper! Duly filled it in and, on the strength of that, was back-classed for three weeks, became a Class Leader and a C.W. (Commissions Warrant) Candidate, which meant that if I was good enough I could get a commission. The remainder of my time at Collingwood I swatted hard as I knew that most of the other C.W.'s had much more time in the Navy than me, many of them with a much better education, and competition would be fierce.

Chapter 14

Passing out of *Collingwood* I was given two weeks' leave and three white hatbands instead of the usual H.M.S. cap tatty, one on - one off - and one in the wash. Irene proudly took me down to show me off to the family along with our small son, Michael. Mother and sister of course were delighted and we all went over to the 'Saxon King' for a few beers. Some of the chaps from Tuckton had pushed *Half-Pint* back to Mother's bungalow, as all craft had to be moved away from navigable waters or immobilized in case of invasion. Immobilizing generally means having a hole punched in the bottom of the boat. I had to listen to hair-raising stories from the neighbours of how they had beaten out the fires around *Half-Pint*, when incendiaries had been dropped.

My leave completed, I took my railway warrant, bag an' 'ammock and ditty box, and joined about forty other hopefuls on No. 3 platform at Kings Cross Station where we entrained for Scotland and *H.M.S. Lochailort*, a shore establishment for the training of Officers for Combined Operations. We were a very mixed crowd, General Service Ratings, Petty Officers, Leading Hands, Artificers, and one or two like myself who had been in the Service for only twelve weeks. We chaps from *Collingwood* hardly knew port from starboard, but we had all studied hard - especially the naval jargon - a completely new language to us civilians. To hear our conversations one would have thought we were real horny-handed, bully-bucko mariners until some 'Stripey' would interrupt the conversation with a remark such as - "I've poured more water out of my bloody seaboots than you lot have ever sailed over!" We would then appropriate the remark for future reference when 'swinging the lamp' (telling tall seafaring stories).

There was no transport from Lochailort Station to the base camp when we arrived, and, as usual in the Highlands, it was raining. The telephone was out of action so one of the senior hands, a P.O., took charge and marched us to the base, along the valley - about five miles away. Loaded with kitbag, hammock, gas-mask, tin hat and ditty box, we set off, blithely enough, and marched to the *Roll Out the Barrel*, *Run, Rabbit, Run*, but, by the time we'd reached our objective, we were struggling along in the dark, a wavering line of dejected figures, No. 1 bell-bottoms caked with mud, soaking wet, and all wondering why we hadn't joined the R.A.F. We were halted at the main gate by a grinning sentry who called up the C.P.O. of the guard. He ambled out of the Guard Room in long black oilskins, a Sou'wester hat worn back to front and carrying an old paraffin lamp. "He looks just like a bloody penguin," I whispered - a name which stuck to him for the remainder of the course.

"Oo-are-yer?" he snarled. "New intake from Portsmouth? Some bugger must know summat, but they didn't tell me nothink! Dump yer kits down 'ere and get fell in. An' let me tell you - them wot's keen in this place gets fell in previous! Right!"

Lochailort was definitely a cramming course, especially for the likes of yours truly, as it was assumed that we all had a working knowledge of H.M. Ships. The only naval craft I had ever been on was a thirty-two foot pulling cutter in Fareham Harbour. Whilst at *Collingwood* we had to learn seamanship, navigation, meteorology, morse and semaphore, shiphandling, arms drill, naval etiquette (very important!), power of command etc. At all times when not under a roof (t'ween decks) we had to 'double'. Daily we did the assault-course, climbed 1,500 feet up the mountainside before breakfast, then we had a five-mile run later to help it down. P.T. and unarmed combat was taken under the eye of a Royal Marine Sergeant who had positively no sense of humour. He also organized the boxing-bouts between the different divisions. I happened to the one of the 'volunteers' who set up the boxing ring. Four padded posts were slotted into the concrete floor of the gym and fitted with ropes. We then rolled out what I thought was a worn Persian carpet. It was only whilst smoothing out the wrinkles I found it was canvas covered with bloodstains. I ask you! The idea was that two men of about the same weight from different divisions were given gloves and told to fight - and no malingering.

That night I was swatting up the Manual of Seamanship when someone said, "Hello, Northy," and, looking up, I saw one of the chaps from the same hut as myself. "See by the notice-board you are down to fight Paddy O'Hara tonight - yes?"

Nodding absently I said, "Yes, nice lad, our Paddy."

He gasped. "Oh Blimey, North! Haven't you heard?"

"Heard what?" - I was suddenly all agog.

"He was Northern Ireland's Light Heavyweight Champion last year, before he joined up."

"No!" I said. "You're kidding!"

"Kidding am I - poor old Northy - you wait and see!" He wandered out leaving me all shook up.

Unknown to me until the following day, he then nipped into the next hut. "Paddy me-old-mate," he said, "got a fag?" Whilst Ordinary Seaman O'Hara was fumbling down the front of his jumper for the makings, John Willie said -

"I see you are to fight Northy tonight at 12½ stone."

"Right, me boyo," said Paddy. "Noice auld feller, Northy - we get on well we do - we do!"

"Well, you won't feel that way tomorrow, old son, " said J. Willie. "Didn't you know he was Northern Counties Champion last year? Oi, oi, oi! Never mind, Paddy - thanks for the fag!"

That night, the gymnasium was dark except for the floodlights over the boxing ring. The Training Commander sat on a high stool alongside, smoking a cigarette in a long holder. He was a right sod - had never been known to smile. Paddy and I sat on stools at opposite corners trying to avoid each other's eyes. The commander looked at his watch. "Fight!" he said. "And let's see some blood!" Charming.

Dong! went the bell and we trotted out, touched gloves and glowered fiercely, sidled and jumped around, weaving and dodging and taking ineffective pokes at each other.

"Get on with it!" snarled the commander. "Get stuck in!"

Dong! went the bell for the end of the round.

Harry, my second, an ex-Metropolitan policeman, whilst dolefully fanning me with a towel whispered, "Northy - stick out your left - just to please me. 'Cos if you don't, and we lose, I'll thump you!" He was about six feet four inches tall and built like a tank. "Our division is two points down already. Right? Stick out your left!"

Dong! Second round.

Whether I was more scared of Harry than I was of Paddy, I don't know, so I danced smartly into the ring, stuck out my left hand, Paddy races up, smacks his chin on it, and falls down!

"Hooray!" yells our division. "Good old Northy!"

"Quiet!" yells the D.O. scowling around.

Paddy climbs up to his feet, shakes his head and charges again! I'm very quick, as you now know, and I thought, oh well, and I stuck out me left hand again. Thunk! Paddy smacked his chin on it again - and fell down again! Twice more in that round it happened!

Dong! End of second round.

Burst of applause from our side.

"Silence!" yelled the commander again.

I swaggered back to my corner where Harry was grinning from ear to ear. "Don't try anything else, mate, for Gawd's sake," he said. "Do it every time he comes up."

I did!

I won! And was held in great respect by all our division. "Killer North - the Yorkshire Earthquake!" All except Harry who smiled a little smile and said nothing.

I got full marks for sailing the old whaler, I'd done that before, of course, in the Sea Scouts. But navigation, ugh! Using a sextant for the first time, I plotted the boat's position slap in the middle of the Inverness churchyard. Theoretical navigation - not a clue! Question: If it's high water at the mouth of the Yangtse River - what is the state of the tide in the Heligoland Bight? As if I cared. Morse: I got ninety five percent - We all did! Probably because the Chief Bunting Tosser had been heard to say offhandedly that he had lost his exam answers. But 'appen - they were in the notebook he had left on the classroom table. It cost five bob each but it was worth it. Seamanship, arms drill, power of command and P.T. seemed to be okay, but the interview was the dreaded part of the whole course.

Came the day, we sat in a line of chairs all trying to look unconcerned. Anyone failing the examination went out of the room by another door, picked up his kit and was taken down to the Railway Station to catch the next train south. He was not even allowed to speak again to his former classmates.

"North F.S. PJX 388864."

Gawd! That was me already! I rose, crossed my fingers and stood outside the dreaded door.

"Best of luck, Northy," whispered Harry. I winked and gave him a warm smile, wondering if I would ever see him again.

"Come!" said a voice from inside the room.

I took a deep breath and marched in.

"Off cap," someone barked.

"Stand on the square."

Standing to attention on a white square painted on the carpet in front of a long table I looked hard at the wall behind and I remember thinking, what a stupid thing to do - put paint on a good carpet.

"Stand at ease - easy."

Letting out my breath, my eyes flicked quickly along the table. My Divisional Officer - two and a half stripes R.N.V.R. - Right bastard he was - he'd sink me if he could. The C.O. - four rings. He was like God. I'd never even spoken to him. Right in front of me was a vice-admiral with a bright red face and a strawberry nose. Bet he's never tasted gin in his life, I thought. A pause.

"Did you wipe your feet before you came in?" said the training commander.

"Yes, sir," I said, again looking at the wall. "The mat had a green stripe and R.N. printed on it."

"Do we have a wooden door knob?" said a voice.

"No, sir, a brass one, and it needed polishing." We had been put up to this by one of the P.O.'s - bless his old heart!

"Now, North," said the Admiral, "you seem to have done quite well considering - er - um - er —."

Considering what? I thought.

"Boat work very good. Meteorology? -m-m-m! P.T. Excellent! Made a good job of your boxing too I see. Power of Command. Good. Morse and Semaphore? Excellent (aside - "Remarkable - this class all have ninety-five percent for signalling! Most strange!") Navigation - Not so good. Theoretical navigation? What! Bloody awful! Let's see, North" - he thumbed through my papers. "You've got a boat of your own, I believe?"

"Yes, sir."

He looked up at me. "How the devil did you manage to navigate? Eh! Eh?"

There was a split second of silence.

Then I bent over the table and looked him square in the eye.

"Sir," I said, "I think the Good Lord who looks after drunks and sailors has been keeping his eye on me! I've never had any trouble getting to my objective! Sir!"

And I came to attention and looked at the wall again.

"What! What! What!" He gobbled like a turkey cock. "What! - Outside! Out of that door!" pointing to the one through which I had come in.

"Wait there - 'strordinary! What!"

I did a quick about-turn and stepped through the door, closing it behind me. I knew I had won. I just knew it!

"Eh, look - bloody old Northy's back," Tony Cowper whispered.

"Shh!" I held my finger to my lips. "Shh, Shh!"

There was a murmur of voices from inside the room.

"Come," said the voice again.

I entered and stood to attention on the square.

"Stand at ease. Easy."

The admiral took a deep breath. "Well, er, North," he said, "we've been discussing your aptitude as a Naval Officer, and er - well, dammit! You must brush up on your navigation!"

"Congratulations, Sub. Lt. North!" - then he smiled and shook me by the hand. (I said he was a nice old feller, really!)

I think, I really think it was the proudest moment of my life. Sub Lt. North. R.N.V.R.!

The training commander walked around the table, grinned and stuck out his hand.

"And the best of luck, young feller - come to the wardroom later and we'll have a noggin!"

It was then the thought hit me. This was the Royal Navy.

It didn't matter to him whether I passed or not, but, if I couldn't take what was dished out - I wasn't in a position to dish it out myself! Or to quote the old saying, *Non illegitimi carborundum* (Don't let the bastards grind you down).

Chapter 15

Again, a couple of weeks' leave. I'd lost a stone in weight and had never felt so fit. We were all allotted eighty pounds in which to buy uniforms. It wasn't enough. I looked at beautiful overcoats offered by Mr. Gieves then eventually bought one at half the price from an old Jew in Queen Street, Portsmouth. I was entitled to wear a sword, of course, but they cost an arm and a leg. However, I did pick up a tatty one in a junk shop in Pompey for three pounds ten shillings. I wouldn't have worn it at Buckingham Palace but at least I did have a sword. Irene whisked me off to meet all of her rich relations, and I took Mother and Nancy to the Pavilion in Bournemouth - again to show me off in all my glory - one Navy ring.

Sadly, in my absence, I had lost some good friends. Sgt. Pilot Willie Williams had been shot down and killed in Germany. Ronny Scott, another ex-member of the Rowing Club, crashed into the mast of a German freighter on a bombing run in his Blenheim. I attended the funeral of Alan Coles, ex-G.P.O. engineer, killed whilst flying with the R.A.F. He left a widow and two young children. Sgt. 'Duff' Doughty was killed in Africa whilst with the 8th Army. Nancy had been engaged to him for two years and loved him dearly. He was the one love of her life and never again did she consider marriage. I think that was when war really hit me. Ronnie Hicks (the best fullback the Rugby Club ever had) was shot down over Germany, but came back after three years in Stalag

Luft III. From where we lived, we could see the red sky over Southampton each night as the Nazis bombed the port and its shipping. Food rationing was really beginning to bite. Somehow the wealthier people always seemed to manage better than the poorer ones. Clothing coupons could be bought on the black market. Restaurants kept running. Even petrol was available if one had enough money.

Naturally I had to call at the Telephone Exchange to swap lies with my old chums.

"F-f-f-ranky!" It was Alfie Faithfull.

"Nice to see you, Alfie," I said with a grin.

He never even asked how I was doing.

"You s-s-s-sod, F-f-ranky! You knew all about that I.R.A. sc-sc-scare, - didn't you?"

"Alfie, me?" Looking innocent.

"Yes, you, you b-b-b-bugger! I found a piece of blue ch-ch-chalk in you old overall p-p-p-pocket! Scared the bloody sh-sh-shits out of all of us you did! You'd b-b-b-better come and buy me a p-p-pint of fr-fr-fr-fr-friggin' beer!"

Which I did. Good old Alfie!

Chapter 16

On our return from leave, all our little crowd from *Lochailort* were sent on a Divisional course to *H.M.S. Victory* at Portsmouth. Nelson's old ship *Victory* was (and is) still there in the dry dock in the dockyard. Her upper yards and topmasts had been sent down, but that was the only concession she had made to Mr. Hitler and his bombers. Sod 'em! Fine on the up-roll! Whilst acting O.O.D. (officer of the day), under the watchful eye of a Chief Petty Officer, I had the occasion to inspect the barracks. They really were an eye-opener. Apart from a coat of white wash, the mess and decks appeared not to have been altered since Nelson's day. Literally thousands of sailors were sleeping in hammocks, slung down the length of these huge sheds. Each man was allowed twenty-two inches of swinging room, at least four inches per man more than they had on the old *Victory* - not much though in 150 years! We visited cells where wrongdoers clad only in white canvas suits, were picking oakum, another of Nelson's punishments. Each prisoner was issued with half a fathom of thick, heavily tarred rope. It was as hard as iron and every single strand had to be pulled apart until each man was sitting on a pile of fluff three feet high. What eventually was done with it I don't know, but it seemed an awful waste of time and fingernails to me.

We had to attend lectures daily, everything from gunnery to gonorrhoea. Even the Padre gave us a lecture saying that 'fuck' was not just a bad word, it was stupid. He gave the lecture in the R.N. Chapel, and when he said the word I expected the roof to fall in. It didn't though. I expect the Good Lord had heard it before.

Chapter 17

At the end of our course we were given postings - all of us being scheduled for combined operations. We were told we were expendable. Happy thought! All hoped to get L.C.T.'s (Landing Craft Tanks) as they were the biggest assault craft we had in those days, with a tiny wardroom and separate sleeping quarters for the officers. Some were lucky. Others got L.C.I.'s (Landing Craft Infantry) or L.C.A.'s (Landing Craft Assault) - which meant living rough and being shore-based. I clicked for L.B.'s. "What's an L.B., Robbie?" I asked.

"Landing Barges," I was told. "Thames lighters with a built-in ramp on the stern and engines. They have very good accommodation too, some of them. Not much glamour about them though, they only do about five knots with a following wind. Just the thing for an old gentleman like you though! Me, I'm all for something more spectacular - like a Midget sub. You can get medals for driving those things." He did actually get his medal, too. But it was posthumous, poor chap. Robbie was nineteen years of age.

H.M.S. Manatee to where I was posted, was a converted Butlin's Holiday Camp at Yarmouth, Isle of Wight, and from there I could see Hengistbury Head behind, which, of course, was my home. As we were still a few craft short for making up the new L.B. Flotilla, I was given *H.M.S. Pauline*, a first world war M/L which had been converted into a yacht at the end of hostilities, and then taken back again by the Navy for this war. Given a coat of grey paint, she was used as a maid-of-all-work. I was very proud of my first command. She was about seventy-five feet long, no more than twelve foot beam, with two small Thorneycroft engines, a crew of three deckhands, two stokers and a petty officer. When we had finished painting her, she shone like a button. Running up and down the Solent for stores etc., I learned quite a lot, having no previous experience with engines and their workings. (I couldn't even drive a car in those days.) The P.O. in peacetime was a mate on a big tug, in Hull. I couldn't blind him with science and had no compunction in asking his advice as a professional. This he seemed to appreciate and didn't seem to take advantage of it. I was really lucky. A couple of times whilst we were away from the base he asked if I would like to go ashore for a drink with the hands. However, I always seemed to have some bookwork to do and had to refuse. That's what the Divisional course was all about - "Beware the three-badge A.B., don't drink with the hands, and he knows more about the Andrew than the Admiral."

I wonder how many reading this story will remember the *Voyage of the Girl Pat?* - and her skipper, Dod Osborne? Just before the war a Grimsby fishing boat was stolen and shipped out of harbour, down channel and into the Atlantic. This was in the 1930's. No reason was ever given, but many years later, it turned out that a man had been killed in a dockside brawl and too many questions were being asked. The *Girl Pat* disappeared into the south Atlantic and half the Royal Navy was looking for her. Eventually she was found, the crew brought back, and they all received prison sentences. The *News of the World* carried the story for weeks. Tales of kidnappings, mutiny, fighting off strange monsters in the Sargasso Sea, Devil's Island - you never heard such a load of codswallop! Anyway, it made her skipper, Dod Osborne, famous. He wrote a couple of books, gave lectures and he even went to the States, talking on radio about it. (No telly in those days.) Anyway, who should turn up at *H.M.S. Manatee* as Boats Officer? Right! Skipper Dod Osborne, Warrant Officer R.N.R. One day he made a bet in the wardroom that he would push the Commander into the 'oggin - and he did. Accidentally, of course. Then he dived straight in to save him and got a Recommend from the Captain. Later, a new Wren Hall Porter was installed at the Base. She was a big girl! As Dod and I walked into the mess at lunch-time he dug his elbow into my ribs.

"Northy," he said. "Look at that piece of crumpet! Cor! Get a load of those titties!"

"Skips," I said, "she'd bloody well eat you! Look at the size of her!" She was a very big Wren, more like a vulture.

"What!" He tipped his hat over one eye and leered at her as she walked past. "Wanna bet?"

That evening there was a clumping of feet on the deck above, and who should clatter down the companion-way but Dod.

"Hi, Northy."

"Hello, Skips - what's to do?"

"Oh, nothing really - just thought you'd like a drink." He pulled out a bottle of Black and White and picked up a couple of glasses. "Going ashore tonight then, Franky-Boy? There's a good picture on in Totland cinema."

"No, I don't think so, Dod, I've just started a rather good book."

"Aw, come on, Northy, be a mate, bugger off for a couple of hours - I'll leave the bottle."

"You haven't nailed that poor girl already have you? You old sod."

He leered knowingly and slurped at the scotch.

Needless to say, I went to the cinema that evening. Later on that night the P.O. met me at the gangplank, saluted me, and said, "Sir, Mr. Osborne came aboard earlier tonight with a lady, er, a Wren."

"Really," I said, looking surprised.

"Yes, sir, and the commander came down about half an hour later and caught them in that little bath of yours." He rolled his eyes and walked away.

I went down to my cabin and looked at the bath. It wasn't any more than four feet six inches long. They couldn't have! It wasn't big enough. It must have been! Dod was confined to his cabin for a week and the Wren was never seen again.

Chapter 18

We did get our complement of Barges eventually and very reluctantly I had to relinquish my command of *H.M.S. Pauline*. Our Flotilla Officer was a Lt. R.N.V.R. by the name of Goodman, not a very apt name as it turned out. He, of course, was always known as Benny. Each officer had a subdivision of three craft with their crews. The L.B.E. (Engineering) had good accommodation for twelve hands with fixed bunks (no hammocks), and a two-berth cabin with shower and w/c for the C.O. and another, in my case an R.N. Equipment Officer. Some L.B.E.'s had a bulldozer or a crane on board, mine had an army-type workshop lorry fitted with lathe, drilling equipment, power saw, welding gear, separate generator etc. It was shackled to eye-bolts and fixed to the concrete lower deck. The Barge was powered by two big Paxman petrol engines, each turning a right hand screw - which meant that the port engine had always to run at 1000 revs less than its mate - otherwise we just went around in circles. I don't know who thought that one up.

Cooking was done in the forward 'swim' (bow) of the barge on a coal-stove, which made the craft lovely and warm in winter but a bit much in summer. The two toilets were of the Elsan type and emptied overboard. An Oerlikon gun was fitted on a platform on deck and a stripped Lewis machine-gun was carried in the open wheel-box. There was a hinged ramp fitted on the stern with which to unload the workshop wagon (always known as Little Annie Lorry). The purpose of these craft was to set up a base on the beachhead to repair any craft damaged in the assault. Each Divisional Officer had under his command two other barges, an L.B.O. (Oiler) and L.B.W. (Water). This was very necessary, as it turned out. These craft were in the charge of a Leading Seaman with two stokers and one O.D. (Ordinary Seaman). They lived on board the L.B.E. when possible, no naked lights were allowed on the Oilers, and rubber soled shoes were compulsory. Would you believe, one day I caught all three hands sitting on the deck of a petrol barge with a primus stove - cooking sausages! They had eighty tons of high octane fuel just eighteen inches away from them! Each Flotilla also carried a Shipwright officer, electricians, carpenters, and motor mechanics.

We exercised with the Army and R.N. Commandos in Shell Bay, just outside Poole Harbour. Our first three craft were ordered to 'Down ramps and unload vehicles'. This they did as ordered, and one after the other, the barges sank with the weight of their vehicles crossing the ramps. No one had thought of this before, so the brains got together and decided that all craft had to beach stern first and be aground before the ramp dropped. It was, as one can imagine, rather unforgettable with any surf running.

A couple of weeks before D-Day, it was decided that the Flotilla would be inspected by a captain (L.B.) at *H.M.S. Squid* (Southampton). Camouflage was repainted, the Charlie Noble given a coat of black paint. (Why every galley funnel in the Royal Navy should be called Charlie Noble I never did find out.) We turned out of the Solent at Calshot Spit Buoy and into Southampton Water. Eighteen little barges, white ensigns flying, all in line ahead. This is what it was all about! Sea-power! Tradition! Nelson! Francis Drake! The Captain in a Harbour Defence M.L. was cruising alongside. Suddenly an anguished face appeared by my wheel-box. The rating was shouting against the sound of the engines and waving his arm astern. I caught the word 'overboard'.

"Full starboard. Astern starboard engine." L.B.E. 18 swung out of line and the Flotilla steamed on without us.

"Stop the engines!"

"Jones, come here!" I shouted, "and repeat what you said." I was struggling out of the wheel- box with a lifebelt in my hands.

"Overboard, sir," said the anguished voice.

"Who? What's overboard?"

"Shit-bucket, sir! I let go of the rope!"

Can you imagine? What price glory!

Later a signal from Captain L.B. "The Commanding Officer of L.B.E. 18 shall give reasons in writing as to why he turned out of line whilst cruising up Southampton Water etc." Out of the gloom, a voice said unto me - "Smile and be happy - things could be worse." And I smiled and was happy and behold - things did get worse!

Chapter 19

As D-Day approached the whole Solent appeared to be just one mass of shipping. Strange-looking craft - the like of which had never been seen before, crawled out of creeks, river and harbours. Some were rowed, others were under their own steam. There was one extraordinary craft in the centre of which appeared to be an enormous cotton reel with a radius of about one hundred feet. What on earth was it? These hundreds of strange craft assembled like an upturned box of Meccano toys, off Spithead, all awaiting the word Go.

We had a false alarm on June 4th, when scores of craft left England only to be turned back again as the weather deteriorated. L.B.E. 18 included! Surely Jerry must know what was happening! But no. Evidently the R.A.F. with its constant watch over the Channel never allowed a single enemy plane to get a sight of us, and at 3:00 a.m. on June 6th we all set off again.

Benny, our C.O., decided that he would be a lot better off on a trawler than thumping along in a barge. He came alongside my craft in a borrowed launch and ordered me to take the Flotilla over to Normandy, where he would be waiting, having organised everything for us at that end. And the best of British, Northy! That left me with eighteen craft, a small torch with a red light, and a hand-printed chart of the north coast of France measuring (I do not tell a lie!) 12" X 8".

The night was as black as pitch. We had come out of the Langston harbour at dusk and we sloshed up and down amidst thousands of other craft for about five hours with only my little red torch to keep us together. 03:30 I headed due south, flashing again me-little-red-torch and hoping to Gawd the next craft astern was doing the same. There were literally hundreds of craft, from destroyers to L.C.A.'s hammering along and all steaming on the same course (thank the Lord!), all in total darkness, the only lights we could see were walls of phosphorescence as they surged past. The noise from those thousands of engines was deafening. By 04:00 hours we were out of the lee of the island, and the sky in the east was lightening. Gradually the crowd of shipping was beginning to thin out as the faster ones pulled ahead. The wind was south-west against the tide - about force six, so it was decidedly lumpy, the old flatbows of the barges were sloshing up clouds of spray and we were down to about four knots. I could make out a string of barges astern, and hoping that they were my ducklings, I clambered out of my wheel-box and crashed out below on a pile of potato sacks. With my tin hat over my balaclava I snuggled into my old duffel coat, told the P.O. to give me a shake if owt happened and had two hours glorious zzzz's. I hadn't slept for forty-eight hours - and I like my bit of kip. Cookie wakened me at about 06:30 hours with a cup of tea. I assembled all my bits and pieces, shifted my revolver to a quick draw position and climbed back into the wheel-box - telling the cox'n to get his head down.

The wind had dropped to about force four and a half, the tide had slackened off and we were making better headway. Taking up my admiralty toy binoculars, I looked astern. Yes! 16, 17, 18, 19! But I only set off with 18. Way astern of the others about a mile away ran another Landing Barge, with clouds of black smoke pouring out of six tall chimneys. Oh, well, it had to be one of our lot - no kraut could have thought of anything as funny as that. The wind dropped away as the sun came up and by midday we were on our own, steaming flat out at five knots. Hands were piped to dinner and we all had an extra lot.

Later on that afternoon Cookie's mate threw overboard a bucketful of gash - out of which floated an empty bottle, bouncing on the waves. It must have been at least twenty yards away, when, for no reason at all, I pulled out my pistol and took a snapshot at it. Crack - away bottle! There was a gasp from the hands sitting on the ramp astern.

"Cor! Did you see Sir?"

"Kinell! - Snapshot!"

"Didn't know you could shoot like that!"

"Do it again, sir!"

I broke open the gun and blew down the barrel as I had seen it done by Gary Cooper. "No, lads," I said. "We can't waste ammunition at a time like this." Never before (or since) have I ever hit anything, but mention shooting after that and my hands were ready to bet their tots on me!

A couple of hours later an M.T.B. lifted over the horizon on a converging course to ours. Slowing down they came up alongside and the C.O., a Lt. Com. R.N.V.R. leaned over his rail.

"Where are you making for?" he shouted.

"That's a bloody silly question, sir, haven't you heard, there is an invasion on today. I'm not just on my own, y'know, there are two or three more craft up ahead."

He grinned. "Actually, I did hear about it," he shouted. "It was on the B.B.C. news. We deep-sea tykes keep in touch, you know."

"But just in case you might be interested, there are three E-boats a few miles up to the eastwards. Nothing to do with me, of course really, but if I were you I'd go a bit more starboard - just the odd point or two."

"Well, according to my itsy-bitsy chart there are soddin'

great minefields up thataway. And as a matter of interest, where are you going in such a hurry?"

"Portsmouth, chum, as fast as I can. I don't fancy tangling with those boys - they have a reputation of playing rough - could ruin my paintwork! Best of luck!"

He turned, waved to the bridge, the M.T.B. lifted her nose and disappeared in a cloud of spray. My cox'n tried to look nonchalant.

"Er, any orders, sir?"

"Yes," I said. "Let's have a cuppa. Oh - and we'll alter course about fifteen degrees to starboard. Just to please the Lt. Commander, of course."

"We'll have no trouble with mines - we're not drawing enough water." Pooh! Mines? Sissy stuff! As a matter of fact I wouldn't willingly sail over one of those things in a rubber duck!

According to my little chart, we made the French coast at Omaha Beach in the American sector. Destroyers were laying down a heavy smoke-screen a couple of miles offshore. But the row that was going on! Things going bang! Things blowing up! Everybody shouting or blowing whistles! Oh! Mind you, the Yanks always were a noisy lot. So, what would Hornblower have done under those circumstances? Same as me, I expect - we drove into the smoke and dropped our hooks. We couldn't see anything, but there, the Germans couldn't either. First job. Brew up and take stock. I reckoned from my chart (Bless it!) we were about twenty-five miles west of our objective, King Red Beach. Just as I was downing my second cup of tea there was a terrific Ker-rump! Ker-rump! T'owd barge nearly jumped out of the water and the roaring noise afterwards nearly burst the eardrums. Ker-rump! Ker-rump!

Oh! Oh! Lord Haw-Haw (the British traitor who broadcast everything from Berlin) had warned us nightly on the radio what secret weapons Hitler had in store for us. Ker-rump! Ker-rump! Shit and shot and shrapnel! Now what would old Horny do? - Bugger off sharpish! I nipped smartly topside - I didn't even stop to finish my tea, signalling all my craft to up anchor and follow me. Our only means of weighing anchor was by the use of hand spikes on the wooden horizontal capstans, quite a performance really as some of the craft had only three hands. However, the 'crunch' every few minutes helped to speed things up a bit.

The smoke was thinning, the wind had gone light south-west and as we steamed out of the fog, we saw about one mile seaward of us *H.M.S. Warspite* playfully firing off broadsides with her fifteen inch guns over our heads. What it was like at t'other end I don't know but the noise at this end was enough for me. We cruised eastwards along the coast. Some miles along we passed a small inlet, I thought it was a fly on my chart but found it was marked P. en B. - Port en Bason which we found out later was the receiving end of the Pluto pipeline. Further along we spied masts, funnels and upperworks of eight or ten merchant ships up out of the sea.

"They must have had a real thumping here, sir," said the cox'n.

Little did we know that they had been scuttled on purpose and this was the start of the Mulberry Harbour, the ships forming a break-water for the transports inside. By this time showers of landing craft of all shapes and sizes were piling ashore and masses of troops, tanks, wagons, and guns were climbing up the slopes of the beach-head. With the glasses I picked out a large oblong of red canvas situated on the sand dunes - this was our destination - King Red Beach.

Chapter 20

Steaming out towards us came a rather smart cutter with a familiar figure standing aft; he came alongside and hailed us.

"Kinnell, Northy. You took your bloody time, didn't you?" It was Dod Osborne, looking like something out of a pirate film. Tin hat, yellow picnic burn dressing for a neckerchief, guns, daggers, hatchets, binoculars etc. dangling around.

"Well, I wasn't really in a great hurry to get here, Dod. Have I held up the invasion too much then? And how the hell did you get here, Skips?"

He climbed on board in his big leather sea-boots. "I came over with Benny Goodman and Tommy Tucker in a trawler," he said. "Benny is nearly wetting his needlework knickers! He has been threatened with a court-martial for skipping off and leaving his Flotilla. Anyway - got owt to drink?"

I handed him a pocket-flask of rum which I kept by me merely for medicinal purposes. "And where did you pick up that pretty little launch then?" I said. "Twin Brownings, dollops of polished brass-work, and scrubbed teak decks. Even got bloody cushions!"

"Oh well, you know, the Yanks got it - er, sort of loaned it to me. Anyway, follow me inshore - and mind those effing tripod things - they're called Hedgehogs. They are old railway lines. Jerry has wired French shells on top of 'em and they've got graze-nose detonators so for Gawd's sake don't even touch them! Anyway, come on, don't hang about!" and off he went at about fifteen knots, skittering in and out of the Hedgehogs. I passed the message back along the line, and we crept slowly after him, being very careful to give plenty of sea-room to anything poking out of the 'oggin. It was practically high-water when we beached our craft in the allotted positions, below the sand dunes near the village of La Rosiere.

One of the first things I did on going ashore was to check my No. 19, Tail-end Charlie. She was beached about three hundred yards away - still belching out clouds of black smoke. As I walked in her direction I noticed some magnificent cockles - no one had been able to pick them for four and a half years as they were the wrong side of the barbed wire. I thought, I'll get the boys to pick a bucketful - I do love cockles. My "barge noire" was labelled L.B.K. 1. Most of the craft was covered by a big iron box-like structure with open portholes along the side. Mounting a ladder propped against the hull I climbed on board, to be met by a Leading Hand holding a notebook and pencil.

"Yes, sir," he said smartly, "how many and for which craft?"

"Er, well no, er, - as a matter of fact I wanted to speak to your C.O." and as I spoke a midshipman in blue battledress came through the doorway, mopping his brow. "Hello," I said, "it looks a bit warm in there."

"It bloody well is," he said, "twenty-four hours a day. Can I help you?"

"Well as we came over from Langstone together I just thought I'd make my number ..."

He looked puzzled.

"Yes, I was in front and you were behind," and I explained what I meant.

He grinned and rolled his eyes. "I was so damn sick I couldn't see straight, so the chief hung on to your tail - hope you didn't mind."

"Of course not, but what's an L.B.K. anyway?"

As he showed me around he explained its purpose.

"Landing Barge Kitchen." It was always known thereafter to the men on the beach as The Caff. At that moment hot dinners were being cooked in the vast coal-fired ovens, and later hundreds of loaves of bread. It was designed to answer the needs of the men on the oilers, assault boats, and other small craft where it was impossible to use a galley. By devoting one landing craft to the sole purpose of cooking it was possible to give the personnel hot meals. The Mid. had ten cooks on board and the seamen spent most of the time spud-bashing. Yuk! It wasn't the best job in the Navy, but my word, they turned out to be a very popular crew. Little Annie was driven ashore and a repair base established in the sand dunes, where the tradesmen were to be kept busy repairing props, welding patches of L/craft, and doing general repairs.

Chapter 21

We all settled down to a routine on board and ashore, but the weather gradually worsened and on D+9 it was blowing a full gale and we were sitting on a lee shore. On the Invasion Coast the beaches were long and flat for hundreds of yards from the high water mark, and the waves were building up into high combers as they rolled ashore. Most of the landing craft were anchored by the stern, their ramps being in the bows. They all took a terrific hammering that night, many of them filling up and having to be abandoned. The barges having a 'swim' bow rode it out, lifting to the breakers racing up the beach. The sterns however, even with the ramps up, took a tremendous thumping, but being ex-commercial craft they were riveted and not welded and built for dock-work on the London River, so, although rather uncomfortable, we stayed afloat until the tide ebbed again.

Raising all hands, I sorted out a very heavy L.C.T. anchor cable and we dragged it manually way out to seaward, fixing the outboard end to one of Jerry's Hedgehogs (disarmed of course) turning up and seizing the inboard end around our two forward bollards. Our own anchor was lifted bodily to the full extent of its cable, buried in the sand with a twenty foot section of iron girder across the flukes and then wired on. All awnings were double-lashed, as was the Oerlikon Gun with a french letter pulled over the end of the barrel to keep out the spray. By this time the tide was on the make again, so we washed off the mud, brewed up and waited. A couple of hours later the seas were slamming into us and a lot of spray was flying about, but the bow was lifting beautifully. Good-Oh! Everybody was congratulating everybody else down below when there was a Gawd-awful crash! I dashed up the deck and alongside us was another barge, broadside on to the seas and pounding away at our bow. My first anchor chain parted, then the bolts of both bollards snapped off and we went broadside up the beach. Fortunately the other craft was taking the full punch of the rollers, but we were shipping an awful lot of water.

The C.O. on the other craft was a right twit! (One practice which endeared him to his division was to assemble all hands during the Dog Watches (time off) - they were all bargers, dockers and stevedores. T124X Ratings. Then, wearing a dressing-gown and smoking a Sherlock Holmes pipe, he would read to them from the Works of Shakespeare, declaring that it was good for them to get a little culture.) He was a Cambridge graduate and sported a bright ginger beard (that offended me no end). He was clad in dripping oilskins with a big ·45 revolver strapped around his waist, his cap was jammed over his eyes and his nasty whiskers were soaked with salt water.

"What the hell do you think you're doing?" I yelled.

"My anchor chain parted so I thought I would hang on to you. Sorry and all that, Northy!" His crew were dangling on to wires and stanchions as huge breakers smashed over his barge. "All hands!" he yelled. "Lifebelts on and over the side - jump to it!"

Dry land was only about two hundred and fifty yards away but with big, raging combers in between it looked rather nasty. The ratings jumped over the side - the Catholic boys crossing themselves before leaping in. All except for his young electrician who shouted, "Sir, I can't swim, I'll hang on until we dry out again."

"Over the side!" shouted his Nibs. "That's an order!"

"No, sir," said the young sparkie, "I'm scared, I'll hang on."

"You're refusing to obey an order? That's mutiny! We shoot mutineers in the Navy!" He pulled out his big revolver and pointed it at the frightened youth. "I'll count three! One, - two, er, er - three! Are you going to jump?"

Pause.

"No, sir," said the lad. "Fuck it! I'll stay here!"

"Well then — er. Consider yourself shot!" Tucking his pistol into his belt, he jumped over the side himself.

R.N.V.R. - Really Not Very Reliable.

All hands had been ordered to stow anything of value in the top six bunks, clothes, blankets, personal gear etc. and wedge them in with their kitbags. The electrics, engines, pumps etc. were by now under four feet of oily water. With great presence of mind I managed to salvage a jar of rum from my cupboard - I always thought it would be safer there. We had 'Sippers' all around, all dry fags and tobacco were pooled and three hours later we walked ashore.

The hands were lined up on the beach.

"Everybody here, P.O.?"

"Er - well, - er, sort of, sir."

"What do you mean - sort of?"

"Well, all except Riley, sir." (A red-headed Irish M/M.)

"Where the hell is he then? He was one of the first ashore!"

The P.O. grinned apologetically. "Well, sir, it's like this 'ere. You told us to stow our gear in the top bunks, but when that other craft hit us, Riley's tiddly suit rolled into all that oily water. When we were ordered ashore he grabbed that machete from the galley and said he was going to chop S.Lt. XXX's 'effing head off, sir."

"Oh, quite! And, as a matter of interest, did he?"

He looked rather sad saying, "I don't think he has caught

him yet, sir."

Looking through my binoculars, I saw two little figures running along the top of the sand dunes - one of whom was waving something over his head. S.Lt. XXX, however, had got a Blue for hurdling at Cambridge and it stood him in good stead. Ours was only one of hundreds of craft piled up on the beach. Along the shoreline was a black oil-soaked strip of flotsam stretching for miles. Battered dinghies, life-jackets, clothing, cabin furniture and lots of lumps of raw meat. This latter looked rather nasty until we found out later that the small supply coaster carrying it had capsized further down the coast. All the crews were bedded down under canvas in a 'survivors' camp' established behind the sand dunes. I crawled into my blankets still clutching my jar of rum, drank a tumblerful neat, buried the jar in the sand under my mattress, then slept for twenty-four hours.

Chapter 22

Thirty-six hours later my P.O. and I mustered the hands. All had washed and shaved, of course, still wearing their uniforms whilst the crew of most of the craft were dressed in odd bits of khaki scrounged from the army. I gave a little speech and told them how pleased I was with their labours. They all grinned and gave three cheers for Sir.

"Now then," I said. "How many of you have lost any gear?"

They looked puzzled, and one chap said as 'ow they 'adn't lost nowt, thank you very much.

"Well," I said, "I've lost my No. 1 suit, overcoat, shoes, underwear and all my issue stuff."

Silence.

"Er, sir, I did lose my tiddly suit," said Riley hopefully.

"P.O. Atkins," I said, "make a note of that. Anybody else lost anything?" It suddenly dawned on them.

"Me, sir - all me underwear and me new boots."

"I lost my overcoat, sir."

"P.O., make a list of everybody's lost kit and let me have it. But no gold watches! Right! Not now - later." (They did very well out of it, most of them collected about thirty to forty pounds apiece. I got most of my initial eighty pounds back again. It was worth getting wet for that.)

I cracked a joke then, about Riley and the machete - the man from Albacete, and whilst they were still smiling I made my suggestion: "What about salvaging and cleaning up the old L.B.E. 18?"

There was a unanimous, "Yes, sir!"

Having got their approval I said, "It's not an order, you know, but I think it's a good idea."

"Yes, sir, let's get the old girl steaming again!"

It took about three weeks to pump her out, get the electrics working and give the barge a new coat of paint. With a new white Ensign flying over the wheel-box we sailed under our own steam (one engine) into Mulberry Harbour, the only craft of the beach-head Division to do so. We kept together as a crew whilst other ratings were farmed out as gash-handles to other craft and flotilla. It wasn't long before our Flotilla Officer (Benny) came on board. I hadn't seen him since D-Day, would you believe!

"Very good, North," he said. "Nice work. Er, did you happen to salvage any jars of rum? Of course it all has to be credited - a lot of paperwork for me."

"Bloody sorry, sir," I said, "but all the jars were broken in the gale," and I produced three broken jar tops - still sealed, that I had picked up on the beach.

The following day I went on board his craft, having heard that the barges in harbour had fresh stores on board, whilst we on the beach lived on compo rations - these were no doubt very health-giving but - yuk! As I went down the companion it looked like Sainsbury's, cross my heart! Boxes of tinned fruit, salmon, crates of eggs etc. were stacked up against the bulkhead, and as I entered Benny's cabin I hit my head on a ham hanging from the deck-head.

"Hello, Northy," he said, putting down his gin behind a pile of papers. "I'm glad you've come, we were just sorting out the decoration our flotilla has been allocated."

"Lovely," I said, "and what have you got - a V.C.?"

"No, but really though, as I am the Flotilla Officer I thought I should have a D.S.O. There's a lot of work gone into it. Tommy Walker thought so too - didn't you, Tommy?"

T.T. was his chum, the engineer officer.

"What did you get, Tommy?" I said with a grin.

He went rather red and mumbled something about a D.S.C.

"We've allocated all the other medals, I'm afraid," said Benny, "except this Oak Leaf - a Mention in Dispatches - I'll put you down for that if you like."

(I'm not fibbing, this was a perfectly true conversation.)

"That's very thoughtful of you, chum," I said, "but give me about ten pounds of that bacon, about four dozen eggs and some of your bloody ham and you can stick the Oak Leaf up your arse! My chaps have been living off compo all the time we've been on the beach! And what about my spirit allowance whilst we're about it?"

"Aw, don't be like that, Northy - of course you can have some bacon - you lot deserve it! The er - er - spirit allowance hasn't come through yet though - has it, Tommy?"

Mumble from T.T.

"Anyway, I'll give you a bottle of my gin, I - er - it's one of my last month's allowance - I - er left over!"

Lying sod! I only hope when he inserted the Oak Leaf as I suggested it had a few acorns on it!

Chapter 23

When we were in the harbour we had a new port engine fitted and whilst this was going on I inspected the Mulberry. It was a D.I.Y. job built on the open beach in front of the village of Arromanches. The Germans, knowing that an invasion was inevitable, had banked on the Allies taking a deep-water port as first priority - Cherbourg maybe, but most likely Boulogne, Calais, or Dunkirk, and accordingly, these latter ports were greatly strengthened, most of their armour and crack troops held in reserve for that purpose. Instead we took our own harbour with us. Churchill himself is credited with the idea. Initially, about twenty merchant ships were scuttled bow to stern in a great semi-circle offshore. Then from D-Day onwards, strange-looking ships were towed over and placed inside the circle. These were huge 'boxes' hundreds of feet long, made of concrete and weighing thousands of tons each. When in position four 'legs' were lowered to the seabed and each 'box' floated up and down according to the tide, giving sheltered anchorage inside for the hundreds of craft needed to supply the invading army. The idea of the modern oil-rig is copied from Mulberry Harbour. Inside the port, long floating ramps were installed - pontoon bridges were hinged together, anchored each side. These were connected to wide floating concrete platforms of sufficient length to berth a freighter. A continuous column of U.S. trucks moved along the leg of one pontoon, loaded from the ships then returned down the other leg. The drivers were all black G.I.s, invariably smoking cigars. It is astonishing that this colossal mass of equipment had been constructed in secret in factories, rivers, harbours, and workshops all over England. And nobody had any idea what they were installing until all was assembled on the enemy shore.

Chapter 24

With the new engine installed L.B.E. 18 was ordered back to King Red Beach again to pick up our anchor and cables, and collect Little Annie who was still in the sand dunes under guard.

"Might as well drop your hook and hang about for a few days, Northy," said Benny. "There won't be much to do as the troops have moved inshore. Just odd jobs. I'll make sure you get your rations - and if it starts to blow - come back here. Don't be caught out again!"

Saucy sod!

We dried out on our old mooring at H. Water the following day, quite happy to be back on our bit of beach again. The L.C.T. cable was still shackled to the Hedgehog with both my bollards dangling on the other end. So, taking them off, we fastened the inboard end onto our old horizontal capstan and seized them with hemp so that, in a hurry, it could be cut.

The Canadians were coming ashore, thousands of them. "Good old Canucks," our boys were shouting. "Give it to 'em!"

"It's all right for you Navy buggers," one shouted. "Your job's finished - we've got to march to Berlin on our own flat feet!"

"At least you didn't get your bloody feet wet - you should have brought your sled dogs to pull you!" etc.

Along with them came the first Free French A.T.S. What a cheer they got!

The R.A.F. were bombing Caen a few miles inland. For hour after hour they streamed over our heads as the old town was pulverized. When the bombardment ceased our infantry attacked, only to be met by a hail of fire from the Jerries. I hated their regime but they were magnificent soldiers. One day I sent Cookie out for a bucketful of those great big cockles, only to find when they were cooked that they all tasted of diesel oil. Such is war! No cockles!

At dusk one evening I was having a quiet pipe on deck idly watching some R.E.s scratching about behind one of the enemy's concrete bunkers. Suddenly there was a Whee! Whoop! Whee! as tracer and incendiary bullets started to poop off skywards. Evidently they were blowing up an old ammo dump. Trails of red, violet and orange tracer soared up into the sky. Better than bonfire night! Lovely!

Suddenly, Ker-rump! Something must have touched off the Big One. About three hundred tons of concrete and high explosive went heavenwards - lumps of scrap iron whistled overhead. As I said before, I cotton on very quickly and I thought "Oh!" and ducked behind the nearest object. Shit! Shot and shrapnel was whistling all around. There was a tug at the leg of my pants. Slowly the noise died away. Silence. Then everybody started shouting at once. I took a deep breath and took stock, I was afraid I might have broken my pipe - this sort of thing could be very dangerous. I found that I was bent down with my bum in the air behind a small ventilator - very vulnerable. My pants were torn, my leg was bleeding and a piece of shrapnel about three inches long was embedded in my calf. I couldn't even feel it! But nevertheless this was IT! I had fought AND bled for my country. What! I didn't bleed much really, but I did bleed. Just think, if I had been a G.I. I could have got a Purple Heart for that! Waal, Whadyer Know! "Aw shucks!" For years I kept that piece of shrapnel on the mantelpiece hoping that someone would ask what it was. They never did. My wife finally threw it away.

Caen was eventually taken and the Germans pushed back to Falaise. Things quietened down and an E.N.S.A. Group arranged to play in Bayeux and Ivor Novello was due to perform. The cox'n asked me if the crew could take Little Annie and go to the show.

"Good idea!" I said. "Sling a hammock fore and aft for me and I'll go with you - if the chaps have no objections that is."

"Fine, sir," said the cox'n, knowing full well that there would be an extra tot in it somehow or another. It was a very hot evening when we left the beach with thunderheads building up in the west. The road, of course, having been under shellfire for weeks was in a shocking condition, the German MINEN signs had been removed so we knew that the verges had been cleared, and my hammock swung happily as we crashed over the potholes.

Turning the hands loose when we got to Bayeux, they promptly dived into the nearest Caff for a few jars of Calvados before the show commenced, and I wandered off to have a look at the town. Surprisingly, there was very little damage to be seen. I wandered into the Hotel Leon D'or and had a glass of wine with the news correspondents. This place evidently was the base for the boys from Fleet Street and they were all drinking beer and swapping lies. Finishing my drink, I said "cheerio", and started back, looking for the big marquee in which the show was to be held.

"Hi, Lootenant!"

I turned to see a rather chubby U.S. Army Major waving to me from across the street.

"Say, Lootenant," he shouted. "Where's the Cunt House?"

Coming over all Navy Blue and Gold, I said in a very English B.B.C. voice, "I beg your pardon, Major."

"Shit! Fer - Cri Sakes! The Goddam Cat House - where is it?"

"Ectually, sir, I'm not awfully certain, but I did see a crowd of you G.I. chappies queuing outside a rather large house further down the road."

"Waal - Waddyer know! I'm in back o' the line again. An' me afeeling like a stopped-up jack rabbit! Adiosy - " and he trotted quickly down the road. 'Strordinary!

The E.N.S.A. show was quite good, but when Ivor Novello, the star, terminated the performance by singing some of his own works, accompanying himself on the piano - *Gathering Violets in the Spring Again*, and other rather sugary love-songs, the audience began to dwindle rapidly with *sotto voce* remarks such as 'Poofter', 'Queer as a trout', 'Oh, Ducky', 'Brownhatter', until his tent was left with the three front rows of embarrassed officers all feeling sorry for the poor chap.

The show over, I walked back to the wagon, climbed into my hammock and waited until the perspiring P.O. collected his flock - all singing "I'll gather 'effin violets", with suitable feminine gestures, and we started off back to the beach. Then it rained - how it rained! In the thunder and lightning barrage-balloons, flying high over the beach-head, caught fire and crashed down in flames - much to the delight of Jolly Jack who gave a lusty cheer every time it happened. We counted ninety-five blazing balloons that night and all agreed it was the best evening out they'd had since they left Pompey. Balloon wire was scattered all over Normandy and the R.A.F. boys had the job of collecting it - orders from the 'Brass' it was fouling up the tank-tracks.

"Brylcreem Boys! Serve 'em right - they shouldn't 'ave joined!"

Photographs

Frank North, 1942

Guests and crew

Sailing holiday on 'Rozita' in Dartmouth

Always drew a crowd

Small crew on 'dog watch'

*First cruise on 'Moneta',
April 1949*

Sylvia and Frank

Guests on early exercise

Alongside at Christchurch

Guests enjoying the sun

Frank and guests

'Yolande' 1947/48

The Dartmouth Boatel and dinghy pontoon

'Charlotte Rhodes' alongside Boatel at Dartmouth from where the BBC filmed Onedin Line

Dartmouth Boatel

Western Night at Cawsand Boatel. Frank lynches an R.N. member

Cawsand Boatel

Mexican Night at Dartmouth Boatel

Western Night at Dartmouth Boatel

The Spanish Bar, Dartmouth Boatel

Frank, Sylvia and crew

Frank's boat, 'Elaine', 1962, Dartmouth

Frank joins Blackpool Sea Scouts, 1930

Frank North, 1993

Chapter 25

One day I found a lovely little twenty-five foot Yankee motor cutter. Everything was made of teak, hull, thwarts, gratings, even the floor-boards. It was floating off the beach-head. All bollards, cleats, etc. were made of brass. She was a little beauty. Findings - keepings, I thought, and had it towed in and made fast to our buoy. All I had to do now was find a way to get it back to the Solent. Cor! There was an onshore breeze a couple of evenings later and one of the seaman thumped on my little wardroom door. "Sir, that little cutter of yours has broken adrift and is blowing onto the beach."

Grabbing my cap I leaped into our dinghy and started to sail ashore. Just above H.W. mark the R.A.S.C. (Boats) Company had a compound in which they stored and repaired their own craft. I looked over my shoulder, and as the cutter hit the beach the barbed wire compound gates opened, two files of squaddies doubled out, and with about fifteen men each side, a sergeant shouting the time, they slid it up the sand into the compound and shut the gate. Thieving sods! My dingy grounded and I ran up the beach. I was furious!

"Sergeant," I yelled, "I demand to see your C.O. at once!"

"I'm here, laddie," a voice said quietly. "Don't shout." And the major in charge slipped through the gate which closed behind him.

"That's my bloody cutter you've just waltzed inside!" I shouted. "What's the game?"

"It's no game, old chap," he said soothingly, "and it certainly isn't your boat, it's mine. I'm going to take it back to the U.K. and make a cabin cruiser out of it."

"Who says it's yours?" I shouted.

"Those two bayonets," he smiled and pointed to the grinning sentries at the gate. "Want to make something of it?"

I'm noted for my quick repartee, so, quick as a flash, I said, "Assholes!" and walked back down to the beach.

My two chippies always seemed to be making boxes and crates in their spare time. These, I found out later were for 'rabbits' - the term for perks - in this case spoils of war and other ill-gotten gains. German helmets, 'Achtung Minen' signs were very popular and, for some reason, Luger pistols. Not to be outdone, I found an old Oerlikon gun-sight box, and under the grey paint it was made of teak. Scraping and varnishing it I took off the iron straps and corner pieces, replacing them with brass and fitted rope grommets in place of the old handles. Inside the lid I painted the usual mermaids and sailing ships. One of my seamen in peacetime was the mate on a sailing barge and under his careful eye I made a model 'spritty' which, sitting on my new sea-chest made my little cabin quite homey. Oh, didn't I waste my time!

Chapter 26

Whilst walking along the beach one evening, I met and spoke with a Free French Air Force Officer, Captain Jean le Breton and his companion, air cadet Michel Colmant. Paris had been liberated ten days previously and they were trying to get organised and start again. However, they had no food, tools, gasoline or blankets so they had borrowed a big truck (First World War vintage) and were quite unashamedly on the scrounge for anything that might help their outfit get moving. Fortunately they both spoke very good English as my French was limited to *basse mer* and *plein mer*. I invited them on board the barge for drinks and suggested that they stay the night with us. This they did and their two sergeants kipped in with the hands on the mess-deck. The following morning the cox'n filled up all their petrol cans from one of our barges. Cookie dug out all our old compo rations - and was glad to be rid of them. Cans of bully beef, boxes of soap, sardines, dried egg - anything we didn't want was gratefully accepted, their country having been occupied for four and a half years anything we could offer was a luxury to them. We were having coffee when Jean said, "Frank, nothing is happening here on the beach now - why don't you come back to Paris with us and meet our families?"

Midshipman James Jarman who was with us at the time thought it was a brilliant idea, especially as if anything went wrong I would have to carry the can. "Come on, Franky, let's have a bit of leave, mate - Benny will never miss us - he never leaves the bloody Mulberry. What about it, eh?"

I was outvoted. Four Frenchmen and one midshipman. It was on!

"What else shall I need then?" I said.

"Bet you couldn't get some more of that white bread we had last night," said Michel, rolling his eyes.

"Organized," said I.

We had snifters after coffee, then I climbed down the ladder to have a word with the C.P.O. cook on the L.B.K.

"Chief," I said, "can you let me have a few loaves of bread by 07:00 tomorrow?"

"How many, sir?"

"Oh - er twenty or thirty."

"Might I ask what for, sir?"

"Well, as a matter of fact we are all going up to Paris tomorrow by wagon and the Parisians haven't tasted white bread for years - you know?"

"Sorry, sir," said Chiefy. "It's against orders and quite impossible as it happens - unless me and my mate deliver it. That would be quite official. Just how far we have to go to the delivery isn't mentioned in the K.R.-A.I.s (Kings Rules - Admiralty Instruction)."

"I quite understand, Chief. Orders is orders. Make that forty loaves and we'll pick you up at 07:00. Right?"

"Right, sir."

There wasn't a smile on anyone's face as he escorted me over the side.

We set off the following morning in their clapped-out old wagon (with no windscreen) a 1914/18 war left over, Captain Jean le Breton, air cadet Michel Colmant, midshipman James Jarman, two R.N. P.O. cooks, two French sergeants and me. Plus all the food and gear we could pile into the lorry. Naturally all the roads had been shot to pieces. Some of the verges had not been cleared of mines so we had to detour quite a bit. It was late in the afternoon when Jean, who was driving, said, "Frank, I know of a farm quite near here where we may be able to get some butter - it's impossible to get in Paris and of course it's worth a fortune on the black market. Do you mind if we detour?"

"Not a bit," said I loudly, using a phrase I'd just picked up off the lower decks. "Fill your boots!"

About ten minutes later, stopping near a farm gate Jean hopped out and walked up the lane. In about a quarter of an hour he reappeared with a young lady who wore a hooded cloak. Both of them were carrying baskets. Jumping out of the cab I was introduced to the young lady. "Margarite," he said, "please meet Lieutenant Frank North of the Royal Navy, a very good friend of mine."

Smiling, she slipped down the hood of her cloak. She was one of the most beautiful girls I had ever seen! Long curly dark chestnut hair, enormous green eyes - they were bigger than her feet! Her figure was superb!

"'Ello - 'ow are you, pleese?" she said, showing more lovely white teeth than any one person should have. Cor! What a cracker! I had been sitting on the beach for weeks and weeks and felt like a bunged-up billy-goat anyways. We all climbed back into the cab with Margarite in the middle and I had to put my arm around her to steady her over the bumps. We trundled along with the two of them speaking rapidly in French, then Jean, leaning across said, "Frank, Margarite lives in Deauville which is only about twenty miles away. We cannot drive in the dark as you know, so she has suggested that we all sleep tonight at her apartment and carry on to Paris in the morning. What do you think?"

I didn't have to think. "But of course! No doubt all the other chaps will be very tired, bouncing about in the back of the lorry." Perfidious Albion!

Jean explained to me as we went along that she and her husband (I thought there would be a snag somewhere!) were working with the Resistance. She personally had managed to get three British airmen back to England through the barbed wire opposite their home, the whole coast having been wired from Cherbourg to Le Havre. We parked the lorry outside her apartment block, her flat being on the first floor. All piled out with the steaming bags and I followed her up the stairs using torches as there was no electricity in the town, Jerry having blown up the power station. She lit candles and we had a drink whilst she called her next door neighbour - another very attractive young lady. Chiefy had brought up half a dozen loaves of bread, so I offered to go down and get some sardines - they hadn't had any for four years! As I went down the dark stairs there was a click-clock of wooden-soled shoes and Margarite came down behind me, slipping her arm around my waist. As I stopped at the door her arm slipped around my neck, and standing on tiptoe she gave me a big kiss. We were just starting a preliminary cuddle when - clump! clump! clump! - down came Jimmy Jarman.

"Sod you, Mid!" I snorted. "What the hell —!"

"Frank, I'm bloody sorry but I've just heard that her husband is due back any minute - thought you ought to know, er - sort of." He grinned. "Flipping good job I'm educated, mate - you didn't know as 'ow I spoke the lingo, didjer?"

We all three went to the wagon and Jimmy climbed in. I patted her bottom, gave her another kiss, and said in my best French what other conquering heroes before had said, "Not tonight, Josephine." - Tubby hubby is on his way back. *Sacre bleu*! As we went back into her flat Jean rolled his eyes, he shrugged his shoulders until they touched his ears. "Merde. It es what ze Ingleesh call ze bloody 'ard lines no?" We were all sitting at the table eating well-buttered bread with sardines and drinking a very pleasant wine when the door opened and in came the husband. I've never seen such a big bloke! He must have been six foot eight inches! There were handshakes and introductions all around. He sat down and over the meal regaled us with tales of life in the Resistance and tales of the Maquis. Evidently he had just returned from an ambush where he and his comrades had killed one hundred and eight Germans. That was a lot more than I had, and all I ever shot was a bottle! We finished our meal with a beautiful Calvados which had been hidden under the wardrobe for four years. Our hostess brought out a portable gramophone, and winding it up, turned to me and asked me if I would like to dance.

"Mais, oui," I said, using up all the rest of my French in one go.

"C'est Anglais - theese one!" And she put on a record of Jimmy Durante singing *Inka Dinka Do*. Not very romantic but she slipped into my arms, we quick-stepped round the room and I gave her a quick kiss every time we passed behind the curtains that divided the room. As we sat down Jimmy said out of the corner of his mouth, "Watch it chum, Old Lofty has his eye on you! If he's knocked off all those Krauts, a couple of Wavy-Navy types is going to be neither here nor there — and I'm only a lad!"

Soon afterwards we turned in. Michel and the two Chiefs in the lounge, Jimmy, Jean and myself (in that order) in the one huge double bed in the best room. The three of us were just starting to zizz when the candle flickered and I opened my eyes to see Margarite bending over me. She was nearly dressed in a diaphanous night-gown, one shoulder strap had slipped off and I could see right down the valley from where I was lying. I closed my eyes and came up like a starving trout for a fly! There was a whisper of silk, and when I opened my eyes again I was looking into the spout of the biggest revolver I had ever seen in my life! It had a barrel the size of a drain pipe! I could see all the shiny brass bullets in the chamber - and King Kong, all eight feet six inches of him, was sneering at me as though I was a Panzer Grenadier.

Jimmy gave a moan and fell out of his side of the bed. Jean said a very rude French word and ducked under the bedclothes, which left me trying to force my head back through the bed-end. He nodded his head - his lips curling to show his enormous fangs!

"Zis revolvaire - I keel many Gairmans wiz heem! Bang-Bang!" - and he poked the horrible thing under my nose. "Ze Briteesh give 'im to me!" and he twirled it round his fingers cowboy fashion.

I was terrified! "Oo yes," I said, "it's a lovely pistol - a really beautiful revolver."

He stood up to his full nine feet and threw the gun from one hand to the other.

I wish he wouldn't do that, I thought. Then he poked it under my nose again. There was a muffled moan from Jimmy under the bed.

"I keel many peoples wiz eem."

He do go on a bit, I thought vaguely. But this is war! This is what war is all about! Perspiration poured down my face!

"Har, har!" he jeered and disappeared into the dark.

Gawd, I've never been so frightened in all my life!

Margarite woke us at 7:30 the next morning with a pot of coffee, explaining that Himself had gone off at about 4:00 a.m. as he and his Maquis lords were to be dropped off in Alsace Lorraine with a radio to keep in touch with our lot and guide them in. Jean said, as we were dressing, that Margarite had said he didn't have a hope of ever getting back. She didn't love the brute anyway, (I was not surprised - I didn't either!) she loved me, and would Jean explain to me that she would wait for me on our return from Paris and then perhaps we could live together. I thought 'lovely!' And then the old North Country "noose" gave me a nudge and whispered, "Aye, but what if he just does 'appen to come back, eh lad?" We walked around Deauville for half an hour before I left, she hanging onto my arm pointing out the boutique and shoe shop that she owned and nodding to the neighbours with a 'Daddy-look-what-I've-got' expression on her pretty face.

Chapter 27

We arrived in Paris the next afternoon and dumped our kit in a small *pension* near Montmartre. Michel then insisted that we visit his home and meet his family who lived near the Madeleine. Madame Colmant made us very welcome with home-made cakes and the first real coffee they had tasted since the Occupation. They had drunk only *ersatz* made from acorns for the last four years. Producing a box full of sardines, tinned salmon, corned beef, sugar, 'tickler' fag tobacco and other N.A.A.F.I. tid-bits, I offered it to her. "No!" she was adamant. No - they were far too valuable - she really could not accept them - on the black market they would be worth a fortune.

"Madame," I said, "I certainly am not going to take them back with me - please, I shall be offended if you don't accept them!"

She thought for a moment. "My family owns a factory and we make perfumes and *maquillage*. If you will accept their black market value in goods that we make, then and only then will I accept them."

A very stubborn lady! We did a deal and I collected sufficient goods to give to each of my own hands on the barge and a pressy from Paris for their wives and sweethearts. That evening Midshipman Jarman wanted to go to Pig Alley. We accordingly went, ending up at the 'Bal Tabarin'. It was much better than the Pavilion in Bournemouth, I must admit, and the following day we 'did' Paris.

We saw the Louvre - it, like many places, wasn't open. Les Invalides and the Eiffel Tower were being used for spotting the snipers left behind when the German army evacuated the city. Near Notre Dame we came across a crowd of people shaving the heads of a couple of girls accused of being collaborators. They were being very badly treated, the other women especially giving them a very hard time for associating with *Le sale Boche*. I personally thought they were working on the wrong people. There were some very smart Frenchmen riding around in big Yankee cars. How come? - and the petrol? Unobtainable! The taxis all used charcoal gas burners with big canvas bags fixed behind their vehicles to hold the fuel. Strangely enough, ninety-five percent of all males had been in the Resistance, or so they said! They all had lapel ribbons to prove it! All very pro de Gaulle! What had happened to the *Melice* and the other pro-Nazi organizations that had been behind Pierre Laval, Marshal Petain and his crowd?

We returned to the beach-head the following day picking up an assortment of refugees along the way. Every hour we stopped for a tiddle - they merely dropped over one side of the wagon, male and female, and 'did it' in the road. *Les Anglaise* climbed over fences and hid in the bushes to have a pee. *C'est habitude. Extraordinaire!* I didn't get back to Deauville unfortunately, because our outfit on the beach had moved into the Mulberry and Benny was doing his nut wondering what had happened to us - and why! As if we cared!

I accordingly moved my lot back again from the beach into Mulberry Harbour and tied up alongside the blockships. Not having much work to do, it was hard trying to find jobs for the hands. In the rubble on the beach a few days previously I had found a flat bottomed pram-dinghy about ten feet long. It was badly battered but I had it shipped on board and turned the shipwright loose on it. Later, making a few inquiries, I found that it had been used by the naval geologists who had been dropped off on the French coast by submarine at night, and the little dinghy had taken samples of the sea bed along our part of the coast with the future landings in view. Chippy made a good job of the boat fitting new planks and a dagger centreboard with a short foredeck and gunwale all around. One of my ex-sailing-barge hands made a lugsail for me out of balloon fabric and I did a bit of sailing around the various craft catching a few mackerel for the cook.

Rummaging through the blockships looking for 'rabbits' (perks) I found a nice compass, a cherub log (which at the time of writing is sitting on my mantelpiece), three lovely little brass gimble lamps, and lots of shackles, rigging screws and bits and bobs which I intended to use on my next boat after the war was over. For about a week we had a corpse abeam of us. Some poor squaddie having failed to make the landing had been found by the Body Snatchers and they must have tied a weighted rope on him, because every day at low water his boots appeared on the surface. It was a bit off-putting first thing in the morning, I must admit. Messages were sent to the authorities, but, before they got around to moving him, somebody had pinched his boots, and then for three or four days two bony feet clad in grey army socks popped up alongside.

Our job, of course, was finished by the end of September, the fighting had pushed on over the Seine, and we were just twiddling our thumbs. We had orders to return to U.K. in *H.M.S. Northway*, L.S.D. (Landing Ship Dock), a vessel then still on the secret list. It was the first mobile floating dock and from it came the idea of the channel ferries. The stern opened up and small craft moved inside. With the watertight Don replaced, the hull was then pumped out and she could get under way. We were all threatened with horrible punishments if anyone spoke of this fantastic new gimmick, but I still have the photo I took with a No. 2 Brownie box camera. The *Northway* landed us at Dover where we moved alongside the old submarine pens, and the ships' companies were sent on leave one watch at a time.

Ronnie Hicks, the best full-back Bournemouth Rugby Club ever had, was shot down over Germany whilst flying with the R.A.F. He spent two and a half years in Stalag Luft III, the infamous P.O.W. camp where about two hundred officers escaped through a tunnel dug under the wire. Most of them were caught and promptly shot by order of Adolf Hitler. Straws were drawn as to who should make the attempt, and Ron luckily drew a blank and stayed behind. He came back with me off leave, lived on board for a few days sailing my little boat around Dover Harbour. I arranged some accommodation for Irene and young Mike, and they too came down to Dover for a week or two.

There were very few hit-and-run raids by the Luftwaffe because the R.A.F. had complete control of the skies, except for the 'Buzz-bombs' -V1 & V2 which came over frequently. But they were all directed at London so no one took any notice of them on the boat. So much for the Nazi terror weapons that were going to bring England to its knees. Most of the squadron had been paid off, leaving S.Lt. David Andrews and myself to hold the fort at Dover. David was an ex-General Service rating who had come up through the 'hawsepipe' to commissioned rank, he not only knew the ropes - he made his own. Having married a Scots girl a couple of years previously they decided they would like to live in Dover at the end of hostilities. It was much nicer than Scotland. With that in view he put a deposit on a little bungalow on the cliff-top.

I had an old service bicycle and I used it to trundle around the dockyard. Dave came up to me one evening and said, "Can I use the old bike?"

"Yes, of course," I said and watched him as he lifted a heavy kitbag onto the crossbar and walk it down the road.

Funny! He walked up to the copper on the gate and said, "Give me a lift with this onto my shoulder, old chap - I'll have to push it all the way home else."

"Certainly, sir," said the dockyard bobby, grunted as he lifted it onto Dave's shoulder and stopped a car to let him through. "What have you got in there that's so heavy, sir?" he shouted as Dave pedalled away.

"Navy Stores, ha! Ha!" He grinned as he walked back to the gate, shaking his head.

I was having a cup of tea one evening when there was a bump on the deck and the old barge took on a five degree list. Funny, I thought, and, going up on deck, found a shiny green S.S. sports car sitting on my starboard fuel tank! A Navy portable crane was standing alongside and David was unhooking two big rope slings and handing them to the driver.

"What's all this about then?" I shouted, as the crane trundled away.

"Sorry about this Frank," said Dave, "but my tanks are about three feet too short to park it - it'll only be for a couple of days."

"Fer Gawdsake — !" I sputtered.

"Don't worry, I'll put a bit of canvas over it - no one will ever know."

By that time of course the crane had gone and there wasn't much I could do about it. He swore solemnly that he had come by it 'onest - "You know me!" - all he had to do was work out some means of getting it out of the dockyard. We had some welding jobs to do on an L.C.T. moored to a buoy in the middle of the harbour, and for the next ten days as we moved about from our mooring, I sweated copper knobs that the Admiral in Dover Castle, who was reputed to spend hours daily looking through his telescope at his flock, would fire a cannonball at L.B.E. 18, or even worse, send for me personally. My hands got quite embarrassed at the ribald remarks shouted at us from other craft - a sports car on board a landing craft - never 'eard of such a thing!

"Dave," I said one evening about ten days later. "It's got to go! Move it!"

"Yes - of course, I'm moving it on Friday night. Don't sweat! You worry too much." This was Monday evening. About 3:00 a.m. the following morning there was a thumping on my cabin door and Dave rushed in. "Get up Northy! Call the hands! Flash up both engines!"

"What? Eh? What's to do —?"

"Get under way, mate, into the harbour - I'll tell you later!" and up he went on deck to single out the ropes.

We steamed out into the middle of Dover Harbour, it was pitch black.

"Stop both engines, Frank!"

I did and wondered what he would do next.

Grabbing a couple of wooden hand-spikes, he, his cox'n and a couple of his hands slipped them under the S.S. and with a 'Heave-Ho' toppled it over the side!

Sperlash! Gurgle - gurgle!

Anyway, if you know of anyone who wants a sports car I know exactly where he can find one!

Every evening when he went ashore, David would pack his ditty-box with groceries, bacon, butter, meat, cheese - all the things that were rationed. One night whilst passing through the gate he was stopped by the dockyard police.

"What do you have in the box?" said the police sergeant.

"Only a bit of firewood," said David.

"Do you mind opening it, please?"

"Not at all," said David. As he said, it contained only firewood.

He made me cringe at the things he did. Fair-haired, round baby face and blue eyes - he got away with murder! We were having a cuppa one evening in my cabin when Dave said, "That's rather a nice writing-desk you have there, mate," pointing to a mahogany chest of drawers with brass handles in which I kept all my papers. "Where did it come from?"

"I dunno," I said, "it was on board when I took over."

"What's going to happen to it when we pay off?"

"Well, it's not on my slop-chit. Everything was written off when we were wrecked over in Normandy."

"Can I have it then, Frank - for the old bungalow, you know?"

"You can have the bloody lot as far as I'm concerned - we'll be paying off in a few days."

"Can I, mate? That's good of you." And he drew out a pencil and started making a list.

It was Saturday afternoon and Dave was standing on the quay alongside a huge pile of strange objects, boxes, bales, mattresses, pots, pans, boxes of soap, brushes, paint, buckets, carpets, a small mangle, folding tables, two wooden forms, and a very nice mahogany chest of drawers. I was standing on deck a few feet below him.

"You'll never do it, chum! You'll need a five-tonner to shift that lot!"

"Oh, I've got one coming any minute now," he grinned disarmingly as a five ton wagon came around the corner and drew up alongside the heap. The driver, wearing a blue Burberry stuck his head out of the window. It was the Commander!

"Hello, Andrews," he said. "I got sick of the office - it's a nice sunny day - I saw your request for transport, so I thought I'd get a breath of fresh air and drive it myself - what do you want to shift?"

"Er - well - this lot, sir," pointing to the heap.

"What the hell is that lot for - a jumble sale? Haw haw haw!"

"No, sir," said Dave, "the old bungalow."

"What bloody bungalow?"

Dave explained as disarmingly as he could.

"You saucy sod! You'll never get that lot through the gate!

You'll end up in chokey!"

"Well, you did ask me, sir!"

There was a pause.

"I wouldn't miss this for the world," said the Commander. "Tell you what!" He took off his hat with the, 'scrambled egg' on it and put it on the seat beside him. Buttoning up his raincoat collar he said, "I look like a civvy driver now - if you think you'll get away with it - I'll drive."

The huge pile of stuff was stacked on the lorry with my bicycle and David sitting right on top.

"Are you coming?"

"Not bloody likely," I said.

"You don't mind me taking the bike, do you? I shall need it to get back again."

"You won't need that, old son, you'll be in handcuffs!"

"Cheerio then" - and with the Commander R.N. driving, off they went.

A couple of hours later Dave cycled back and put a lock and chain on the back wheel.

"It's best to do that," he said seriously, "you can't trust the buggers round here these days."

I was looking at him with my mouth open. "Go on - tell me!"

"Well," he said, "we went up to the main gate and the dockyard police said, 'What's that, sir?' And I said 'Dead Officer's effects' - so he said 'Oh, oh - please carry on, sir,' and waved me through."

That's perfectly true! Scout's honour!

The barges were paid off soon afterward and towed back up the London River where they were born. My second ring came through and I became a full Lieutenant R.N.V.R. I took Irene and Mike back to Bournemouth and, having had a few days' leave, went as C.O. to *H.M.S. Dragonfly*, a converted holiday camp on Hayling Island. As far as combined Ops was concerned the war in Europe was running down fast. V.E. Day came and we all got a bit drunk and Dave and I wondered what we would do next. "What about the Far East?" said David. "I know a bloke at the Admiralty in Queen Anne s Mansions - he may be able to get us a job out there." The thought of Civvy Street, rationing and clothes coupons didn't appeal to us at all. We both went up to London and Dave wangled his way in to see the officer in charge of Naval Appointments. He came out beaming! "We've got appointments as spare officers on one of the new L.S.T.s" (Landing Ships Tanks - a new, much larger, ocean-going craft built to replace the old L.T.C.s). "We go first to Australia and sort ourselves out from there!" What about that then!

I vaguely thought about Australia - Irene might like to go back - perhaps we should stay there? Things were not going too well with our marriage and she might be happier there. These thoughts were going through my mind as we walked down the stairs. We had three hours to spare before we got the train back to Havant.

"Eh," said Dave, "let's go to the Whitehall Theatre and see Phyllis Dixie."

"Okay," I said, "why not?"

Miss Dixie was one of the new lines of entertainment - a strip teaser! We duly went and sat in the front row of the stalls. Phyllis did her stuff! Very nice. Very Sexy. She came out onto the podium over the orchestra on a short gangplank to take her applause. As she walked over our heads she stumbled and her kimono flipped open.

"Cor bloody blimey!" said Dave in a loud mock North Country accent, "it's full of putty!"

She had a tiny white plastic cover inserted in her vital parts. She looked down at Dave and blushed! If he could make Phyllis Dixie blush, you can see what a character I had to work with. As we left the theatre motor horns were blowing! People were shouting! A.T.S. girls were sitting on the tops of taxis, their legs in khaki knickers, waving to everyone and shouting.

"What goes on then?" said Dave. I walked over to a policeman and asked what it was all about.

"Haven't you heard, sir? The Japs have surrendered - completely! The Yanks dropped another atom bomb on them - and serves the buggers right!"

So we didn't go to Australia. *Dragonfly* was closed down soon afterwards. I got my demobilization papers, two hundred and fifty pounds gratuity, and a grey flannel suit with a pork pie hat. I was a civilian again.

Chapter 28

I had a few days' leave, and first tidied up Mum's garden and dug up the air-raid shelter. Then I went down to Telephone House where my job was awaiting me.

"Nice to have you back, Lieutenant ... er ... Mr. North," said the Chief Engineer with a grin. "Any ideas on what you would like to do?"

My sister was now in charge of a department there and we had discussed the question the previous day. "Well, I've heard that there is a new Sales Department opening - I was wondering if I might be suitable?"

"I should think you would be ideal, Mr. North - of course you'll have to work in the office for a while to get acclimatized, but yes, a very good idea!"

The thought of working in an office appalled me but what could I do? As I puttered around Mother's garden one evening I had a bright idea. "Irene," I said, "would you like to live on a boat - a big one? We can't afford a house - that's obvious even if there was one, but a big boat - like my old *Pauline*?" She had been over to see me whilst I was at *Manatee* and was rather taken with what she saw. "We-e-ll - yes - I suppose so - at least we shall be in our own place, and that would be very nice."

The next Saturday I got the train to Lymington, as I had heard that there were a lot of ex-Naval craft over there - for sale. Perhaps *Pauline* was amongst them? Lymington Shipway Boatyard was chock-a-block with grey painted ex-Naval craft.

I asked permission to look around. And there was my old *Pauline* looking very ratty with her bow stuck in a mudbank. Oh dear, she didn't look the same vessel. I mooched around. Old landing craft, motor launches, M.T.B.'s and all with the starch gone out of them. There was a very old converted lifeboat chocked up against the rigging shed. I stopped with my head on one side and looked at her. Something was ringing a bell. The yard foreman came up and pointed with his pipe, "You know 'er, sir?"

Looking at him I shook my head slowly, "It's that false transom stuck on the stern that's foxing me."

"Did you ever read a book called *The Riddle of the Sands*, mister?"

"Yes, why - yes - of course! It's *Dulcibella*!"

He grinned at me. "Yes, it is," he said. "Used to belong to a Mr. Childers many years ago, I'm told. A lot of gentlemen have been over here to see 'er. There was some talk of raising a subscription to have 'er done up again and put on a concrete base like. Don't know if anything will ever come of it."

"Well, you can put me down on your list anyway," I said, "if they do."

The Riddle of the Sands is a classic read by all sailing men, written before the First World War. Erskine Childers was executed in Ireland at the time of the 'troubles' by the Irish. I wandered along the rows of craft.

Stopping to light my pipe I found myself looking at a fat round bubble-bowed boat with a big mast tabernacle which was sticking up on the deck, and wherever one looked there was a curve - not a straight line on her. A Dutchman obviously - a boyer, a botter, or a lemmeraak? I picked up a plank and teetered on board. Everything inside and out was covered with 'crab-fat' (Admiralty grey paint). Water was sloshing over the floorboards. The toilet was bunged with all sorts of nasties. Taking out my knife, I scratched the panelling in the huge saloon - it was oak with a circle of holes where one dartboard had been. There was a big forecastle with a rusty iron coal-stove bolted down, two double cabins and one single. Lifting up the iron hatch in the cockpit I saw a mass of rusty iron that had once been an engine. I shuddered and dropped the lid back. A huge curving rudder about six inches thick with an enormous rotten tiller sticking out of it. Teak showed under the chipped paint of the cabin top, *Yolande* was painted crudely over the converted nameboards on her stern. There was a huge rusty winch alongside the mast tabernacle and winches each side for the leeboards, they too were solid with rust. She was a ghastly sight - and I fell in love with her immediately!

I borrowed some money and, with my gratuity, I bought *Yolande* for five hundred pounds and had a local fishing boat tow her round to Christchurch. That cost a further five pounds. I still have a copy of Lloyd's Register of Yachts, dated 1948, with details of *Yolande*: built in 1904 in Lekkerkerk, Holland, length fifty-two feet, beam, fourteen feet.

After much searching around I found that she had been laid up for the war at Bursledon, at the top of the Hamble River. There I found the remainder of her gear. Mast, boom, leeboards - a lovely gaff with a double curve in it, a curved rudder head, the 'Dutch stroking' for her masthead, ropes, rigging, blocks etc. I bought the lot for another fifty pounds. It took me a year to make her interior inhabitable. The saloon panelling I burned off and scraped. There was an old rusty anthracite stove which I repaired and fitted with a brass chimney. The cabins were white enamelled, the galley refitted with a full size bath under the lifting table top. We were given a lovely big carpet for the saloon and, last of all, we installed the Delft with its pewter plates and bolted it to the bulkhead.

I rented a mooring on an island in the River Stour, just

below Tuckton Bridge, for five pounds a year. To reach it, I chopped down a big elm tree that was leaning over the water, lopped off the branches and made a walkway along it with a wire handrail. The old army pillbox built on the island made an ideal store for all my toys and bits and bobs. Irene, Michael and I moved aboard in the autumn of 1946 and in the winter of that year the river froze and we could walk from bank to bank.

Eddie Mossop Lt. R.N.V.R. tied up his yacht alongside. Her name was *Katwinchar*, and she must have been thirty years old then. He bought her for fifty pounds, rebuilt and re-rigged her and sailed her later to Tasmania. He was a fantastic navigator. Bunny Austin, ex-R.N.V.R., kept his little yacht *Bessie* near the island. *Yolande*, because of her size, became the official meeting-place for all the local ex-service types and we had long, nostalgic boozy parties each weekend. Life had suddenly gone flat on us. The excitement had gone and we couldn't settle down to our civilian lives. Yes, we all had jobs, but none of us had any real interest in them. Rationing, of course, would be with us for the next three or four years. Those who hadn't joined the services were now our bosses and it rankled a little. I loathed my office job - so much so that I developed an allergy. At ten o'clock each morning I would start to sneeze, and for the remainder of the day my nose dripped like a tap. My eyes would get inflamed and I used to go outside in the open air to breathe properly. Every week I would ask to speak to the Engineer regarding my job in the Sales Department. I was put off with, "Don't worry, it takes time - you're doing well in the office."

Our marriage wasn't exactly what I had expected. Irene never loved living on the *Yolande*. She never once lifted a paintbrush or helped me on board in any way at all. Mike started going to the local infants' school and he was quite happy there. At weekends he would stay with my mother and sister in the bungalow. I started to assemble the boat's rigging. The winches were all rusted solid and I worked on them for days, filing all the cogwheels and loosening all the joints with a blowlamp, then soaking them in oil and paraffin. Some of the spindles I had to replace, but eventually I got them all working, painted and ready for use, making covers for them from Admiralty canvas. The mast, boom, bowsprit and gaff were all scraped and varnished and I set up the rigging whilst everything was on the river-bank. Came the day to step the mast: I bought a crate of Huntsman's Ale and all the local chaps were conscripted.

Yolande was firmly jammed with her bow into the riverbank. Lines were rigged aft from Tuckton and to a big anchor down the river. We manhandled the mast into the tabernacle - it was about a quarter-inch thick at the base, stopped with iron and a huge bolt as thick as my wrist was pushed through and bolted on. The mast was pitch-pine and must have weighed well over a ton and a half. Eddie scrambled up a big old oak tree hanging over the boat stern, shackled an iron-bound block about forty feet up the trunk and wove a heavy wire through and back to the winch in the bows. I said a little prayer and started to turn the winch-handle. Slowly the mast rose above the deck, hands on both sides steadying it with the guy-lines. Traffic on Tuckton Bridge came to a halt and crowds of people leaned over the railing giving gratuitous advice. Eddie, still up the oak tree watching, suddenly yelled "Belay!" and as I turned I saw a tiny something fall off the block. The split pin holding the sheave had broken off! The mast was at a forty-five degree angle hanging over the boat - if it had dropped I shudder now to think of what would have happened to my lovely teak cabin-top and deck. Jamming a big screwdriver between the sheave and the side of the block to stop any movement, he gingerly crawled down the tree, grabbed a hammer and "snuck" up again. It's only holding on by an eighth of an inch and he yelled, "Stop that bloody motor boat - its wash could wreck the lot!" He gave the pin a sharp clunk with the hammer and grinned down at us. "For gawd's sake, lads, take it slowly and I'll keep thumping the head of the pin." I turned the winch-handle and the mast started to lift again to the tap-tap of Eddie's hammer. No more frights. It stood upright in the tabernacle and I slapped over the iron clamp and banged in the pin. Olé!

"I don't know why you are spending so much time doing this," said Irene, coming up on deck to see what all the noise was about. "It's only a houseboat anyway, we're not going to sail it - after all, it's my home - what about my crockery and things?"

Wot a sheila! We really didn't agree on lots of things. "Anyway, dear, it does look nice with a mast stuck up there, doesn't it?"

"Yes, I must say I like that little flag thing on top," pointing to the Dutch stocking shifting in the breeze, "but she's a bit wobbly when other boats pass."

Eddie grinned, rolled his eyes and stooped for another bottle of beer. The leeboards were oak and bound with iron. I had to rig sheave legs to fix them. I made a new tiller with a double curve in it and carved it with fishes and mermaids.

One day in a junkshop in Boscombe I found a lovely little six-foot model of a thirty-gun frigate. Ooh! The hull was framed and planked, it had little brass guns, a cutter, jolly boat, everything. It must have taken years to make. During the war it had been bomb-damaged and the masts and rigging were all smashed and heaped on the deck. Everything was there - block, fighting tops, lanterns, rigging, and dead-eyes still with their little lanyards. It just wanted someone to love it and set it up again. "Eight pounds for the lot," said the junkman - I could have got it for six! "No," said my wife, "I'm not having all that rubbish cluttering up my saloon! No! I shall leave you if you bring it here." Just to show what a good husband I was I didn't buy it. Forty years later (when marriage to Irene is a memory) I'm still regretting it!

I still had the little pram-dinghy I found on the beachhead. Irene christened it *Twee*, and I took Mike sailing in it and taught him how to row. The yacht's headsails weren't too bad but the mainsail was rotten. I got estimates from various firms but they were too costly for me. However, I talked with an old sailmaker in Poole. He fished out some bundles of flax canvas he'd had stored since pre-war days and he made me a mainsail for twenty pounds. When it was finished I took it down to the Fisherman's Quay at Poole and had it oak-bark tanned by the boys who were dyeing their nets. It lasted very well. The 'cut' wasn't up to Ratsey's standards but, as it was lashed to the mast with a long hemp line, all the slack pulled out as necessary, and hanging ten inches behind the mast the 'flow' was perfect. Unfortunately when it rained the oak-barking washed out but it ended up a nice orangey-pink colour, so I couldn't complain.

I rigged *Yolande* down and was dying to sail her in the confines of Christchurch harbour, but in the stretch of river in which she was moored, we had to have an engine and I had no money left. What to do? Roy Hobbs was a draughtsman working for BOAC at an airport, but he had served his time on the bench as an engineer. "Lets have a look at this lot under the cockpit," he said one day. We lifted the hatch and crawled down.

"Migawd - what do you say its name was?"

"A French Baudouin. It's about twenty years old, I think."

"I believe you, mate," said Hobbs. "It's got to come out anyway, so let's get the old bugger on the bank and have a good look at it - in theory any engine can be made to work no matter how old it is."

We sawed off the holding door bolts, uncoupled the shaft, exhaust and water pump, rigged the sheavelegs again, and got the rusty heap on the river bank.

"Strip it down to the last nut and bolt - don't throw anything away - and chuck all the bits in that old oil drum. Wire-brush down everything in sight, and I'll come down next Saturday and we'll have another look. And the best of British luck!" said Hobbs as he ambled over the gangplank.

It was just a mass of rust and full of water. The head had been taken off at the beginning of the war and dumped in the bottom of the boat. All craft at that time had to be made inoperable when invasion was threatened.

"Gawd blimey," said Hobbs, "why don't I keep my big mouth shut?" Every nut and bolt had to be soaked in oil and paraffin (no 3-in-1 in those days) and chiselled off. It was impossible to get any spares for it. Even petrol had to be salvaged as it was still rationed. All parts had to be stripped down, scraped, filed and graded. We spent hundreds of hours converting bits from other engines and rebuilding it. I hated the beastly thing! Despite what the R.N. per-si-cologist said, I don't think I would have ever made a motor mechanic.

However, one Saturday evening - having swung the flywheel for hours, I said, "Let's pack it in, Hobbs."

He adjusted his knobs and bits and pieces. "Just one more time, Skips," he said. "If it doesn't go, we'll knock off and have a pint. Right?"

"What a hope!" I said, and swung the flywheel again.

Bang! Thunk! Clunk!

It started! I nearly fell over backwards. Black smoke, steam, oil and petrol vapour squirted out from all joints and couplings.

Bonk! Bonk! Bonk! Bonk!

It kept on bonking like that every time it started for the next three years. But it did keep going! Hobbs stopped all the leaks and squirts. We slipped her gently into gear and she took up the slack on her mooring ropes. Neutral! Astern! Back she came, bless her old heart. I had an engine! What about that!

Irene left for good. Michael went to Mother. When I left the government job I lost my sneezes.

That first season of 1947 I trundled up and down, doing the 'Solent pub craw'. I obviously wasn't going to charter the old boat outright for every week of the season, so I opted for paying guests. "Come for a sailing holiday and help to work the ship" - which involved a bit of cooking and washing up. I did have a paid hand for a few weeks, a chap of about twenty who was as wet as the proverbial scrubber. Three times that season he had me overboard. He said he would do anything a seaman would do! Except go up the mast! He couldn't stand heights! Sorry! I got him in the bo'suns chair under some excuse or other and hoisted him up there. From that day on he was a 'killer-diller' with the girls! He went up the mast three times a day on one excuse or another. Coming on board one evening from the pub in Ashlett Creek he knocked over a paraffin lamp. Instead of stamping out the stream of flame that ran over my lovely carpet he kneeled down and lit his fag from it. Anyway, his mum decided that life at sea was too rough for her lad, would I mind awfully if she whipped him away and got him a safer job on shore. Would I mind? It was school holiday time so teacher Sylvia jumped into the breach as crew and took over his job.

Sylvia Harding - divorced - with a son named Michael, lived on a boat about one hundred metres downstream from my mooring at Tuckton. Michael North was taught in Homefield Junior School - as was her own son. Sylvia ran the Junior School at Homefield.

Best hand I ever had! We ate every day! Just like the rich people! I ended up that summer with a little bag of gold when all expenses were paid, sufficient to see me through the winter with one or two sign-writing jobs to help out, and a few parts in Dirk Bogarde's film *Ill met by Moonlight*. Also, I had time to do some more paintings and the odd carving - some of which I managed to sell. *Gracias á Dios!* Of course

I wasn't satisfied trundling along the Solent - I wanted to go foreign - naturally.

The next season I did Cherbourg to the Hook of Holland, dropping and picking up guests at Shoreham, Newhaven, Dover, and when Sylvia joined me again at the end of July for her holidays we went up the Seine to Paris, up the Scheldt to Antwerp. As we entered Christchurch Harbour in September I had a pair of handmade wooden clogs hanging from the end of the bowsprit. That was sheer unmitigated, unforgivable swank - to impress all the local yachtsmen who had never been out of the Solent. Remember, this was before the sailing boom that built up over the next twenty-five years.

Calling in at Deauville I made an excuse to slip ashore. Naturally I looked up the boutique which Margarite had proudly showed me. On impulse I went in and asked the young girl if Madame was available. "Mais, oui," said the lass, waving a hand and out came King Kong! All twelve feet of him! "Ah, bon jour, Mistaire Lieutenant Anglais! Comment allez-vous?" He didn't look quite as impressive without his revolver, but he was still a very big bloke! I said, "I'm very well thank you - nice to see you got back again," and bowed myself out. I never was very brave anyway!

The last few trips of that season we had a real thrashing - it was a typical English summer. I remember thumping along with a broken lee-board, the gaff-jaws twisted off, and all my passengers seasick, when out of the blue came the Scowegian four-masted *Viking* - steady as a rock, everything drawing - beautiful!

Where, apart from Holland, could one buy a lee-board for a fifty foot lemmeraak? She couldn't sail without it. I found a real Western Ocean seafarin' type near Hammersmith Bridge. He lived on board a big boyer, was always dressed in a blue blazer and peaked cap, and had never sailed out of the London River. He sold me his lee panels.

Yolande made a lovely home, but she was not designed for thrashing across the channel. Her fat old apple-bow was made to burst into the chop of the Zuider Zee in a rainbow of spray. She was dry as a bone but in bad weather she rolled like a barrel. However, the season ended and I was tied up again in Christchurch when I was approached by a couple who lived on little forty-foot schooner. Would I do a swap for their boat (which had a big diesel engine) plus a thirty-foot converted fishing boat and a sizeable cash adjustment? They never left the harbour anyway - all they wanted was a comfortable floating home. It was becoming the 'in' thing - converting M.T.B.'s, landing craft etc. It gave them an air of daring and non-conformism. I accepted.

Moneta was a forty-foot schooner made by David Hillyard of Shoreham. They were made by the mile and cut off to length. Cutters, yawls, ketches, schooners, you name it. All off the same moulds, pick your own rig - engine extra: nine hundred pounds. Makes one think when one considers prices these days. She was ideal, schooner-rigged with a big fisherman topsail, masts in tabernacles, and forty horsepower Ailsa Craig diesel engine, and she would sleep eight in the maximum of comfort. When she went aground she'd sit on her chine and so it was possible to anti-foul both sides. This we once did way up the Scheldt, much to the amazement of the local fishermen. She was a little cracker!

I was beginning to know the ropes by then. The guests on board didn't really want to sail in anything more than force three. They wanted to go on board and check into a different port every night. So! We hoisted her sail as we left port in England, started the diesel and hammered across the channel. If the weather was fine the next morning, we'd trundle along twenty miles down the coast. My customers would each steer a zig-zag course for an hour at a time, then go below, have a beer and talk about it, we'd then dock into harbour and settle for the rest of the day. It wasn't really what I wanted but I had to make a living and it was better than that bloody office!

And the thirty-foot fishing boat? Her name was *Nil Desperandum* - to them wot's not eddicated like wot I am, it means 'Near Despair'. I sold it to a couple of young men, one played a guitar and the other sang and had it off (I've just learned that expression) with ravenous females who wanted to be different. *Viva la différence!* I suggested they learn a little bit about sailing before they ventured outside the harbour. But no, off they went and somehow they broke the rudder (in deep water?). They ended up off the Needles and hoisted the flags 'T.O.W.' meaning, of course, that they wanted a tow. Unfortunately, in the International Code it means 'I am running through ice', which must have confused the coastguards on the Isle of Wight more than somewhat, as it was the middle of August. Never mind, I got the brass.

Crew Sylvia and I once both vowed we would never remarry, not for all the tea in China. We had now sailed together on and off for three years. She had taken over the bookings, organized my (limited) finances and painted bilges. We had got quietly drunk together, she learned all the words to the dirty rugby songs, and she was a smashing mate. One evening, sitting on the harbour wall near the lovely little Norman church at Barfleur near Cherbourg, I asked her to marry me. Silence. She thought about it. Then she said, "Well, someone has to take you in hand. You can't go on living on whale-steak and chips - you'll get ulcers. My son likes you. Your boy likes me."

I was never a very good cook. (To any American who may read this, we in Britain were still on rationing four years after the war finished! *We* didn't get any Marshall Aid - the Germans did! The Japs got millions - we didn't! Do you remember those 1918 four-funnelled destroyers we swapped for the West Indian Colonies? Anyway, they won the war - according to all I have read since, we just helped them out.)

I digress. Me old Sylvia decided, yes, she would marry me. Best thing I ever did! She could do all sorts of clever things like reading, writing, and a-counting figures - and she also looked rather nice in one of those new-fangled bikinis!

Chapter 29

Another sailing season passed and I was asked if I would like to go as skipper on a sixty-foot Bermudan cutter owned by Robert Blackburn, the Managing Director of Blackburn and General Aircraft. They made the Blackburn Skua used by the Navy during the war and were now building the Princess flying-boat at a marina at Cowes. Sylvia thought it was a good idea. I had been offered a good salary and we would be able to have more time together. The owner had plans to take her to the Mediterranean in a couple of years hence. In the meantime Sylvia could come at weekends as cook and spare hand. I lived on *Moneta* and took the job.

Carmela was a lot of boat, designed to be sailed by a skipper and at least two hands. She was sixty feet long and drew nearly ten feet of water. Her mast was eighty-six feet long - I know, I measured it. I brought her round from Lowestoft with a scratch crew and put her on a buoy off Brownsea Island in Poole Harbour. The owner knew nothing about boats. He came down to the harbour the next weekend and suggested we go for a sail. I was appalled. I only had Sylvia and his two little daughters to help. We went for a sail over to the Needles and back. Coming home I put up the big Yankee jib (which ever after he called the American sail). I tried to explain that she was a bit of a boat to handle and we must have at least one other hand. He agreed and said, "Leave it to me - I'll organize it." He never did, and for three seasons we ambled along short-handed. Poole Harbour is not very deep and picking up the buoy was a nightmare. Fortunately it was one of the big rubber ones laid down for the old Sunderland flying-boats that used the harbour during the war. With her draft, she was really only suitable for Southampton or Liverpool.

I did a painting of her under sail and sent it to the family for Christmas. His wife - a real charmer, talking to Sylvia, said, "I propped it on the table and when Robert came in he said, 'That's my yacht - where did you get it?'"

"Franky, your skipper painted it for you."

Evidently a big tear rolled down his cheek. "Why did he do that? I never sent anything to him."

"Perhaps he likes you," she said.

He shook his head. He couldn't understand. People evidently only did things for him for money. The guests he invited on board or to whom he loaned the yacht took him for everything. They drank his gin, ate his food and took the Mickey out of the old chap. It made me furious! One evening he invited me down for a celebration drink.

"What are we celebrating, Guv'nor?" I said.

"I've been a millionaire for a long time actually, but now, as of today, I've heard from my accountants. It's official, I really am a millionaire."

I drank his health, wished him well, and thought, "My God - I wouldn't change places with you for all the gold in the Indies!" Sylvia and I had married after my first year with him, and sitting in the saloon a couple of weeks later he tossed a couple of keys across to her. "What are these for, Mr. Blackburn?" she inquired. He smiled and said, "I don't like you and Franky living on that boat during the winter. I've taken a cottage for you near here. Use it for as long as you like." He was a nice chap!

Carmela had a refit at one of the best-known yards in Poole. The refit was in preparation for a trip to the Mediterranean.

The job was skimped and the work atrocious. The yard foreman had his hand out for perks all the time we were there. All the local skippers took their owner for everything they could. It was stupid. These owners were the backbone of the new sailing boom - as a rule they knew nothing about their yachts - they left it to the professionals. And they robbed them! As I had occasion to say once, "I may not be the best yacht skipper in the business, but, by God, at least I'm honest!"

I examined the huge mast as it lay in the yard. Turning to the foreman, I said, "I gave instructions for this mast to be scraped before varnishing."

"It's been scraped," he said belligerently.

"Well, you can bloody well scrape it again!" I said. "My owner isn't going to pay for that!"

We didn't get on very well, that foreman and I.

Mr. Blackburn had a heart attack and the Mediterranean cruise was cancelled. *Carmela* went to the Royal Navy.

Chapter 30

Sylvia's headmaster made a suggestion. She had built up the junior side of his school and trebled the number of boys there. Homefield School needed to expand. He had all the teachers he required, but wanted a boarding side to the school. Why didn't she and I start one as a separate business and work together with him? Financially it was a very sound idea. As Sylvia said, "We could get a smaller boat and would have the long holidays in which to sail." Besides, she would like to do it. It was a challenge.

"What am I going to do though?" I said, feeling rather bewildered. "I know nothing about kids or education."

"You can be a sort of housemaster and teach them handicrafts, painting, rugby, swimming. They will only be here in the evening - you will have all day to work on your boat. Anyway, our two boys and their friends think you are marvellous. You'll have all the kids in the palm of your hand to start with!"

Of course we had no money, so I sold the *Moneta* to help pay for the new business. We rented a lovely old house in Southbourne with a big garden, quite near the beach. After we had started the new venture I had two hundred and fifty pounds left over, so I bought an old fifty-two foot ex-R.N. Harbour Steam Launch. Her name was *Tuffin*. We had about thirty little boys dumped on our hands from the word go. Sylvia found a good cook, and a house matron. With thirty kids around (which included our own two) she was in her element. She loved it! In the evenings after prep I organised games, taught the boys painting and modelling, and, in the summer, went with them down to the beach.

After taking them to school in the mornings, the day was my own and I would nip down to the river and work on *Tuffin*. We couldn't stand that name, so we called her *Michaela*. That made three Mikes in the family - four with Mickey Dripping! She was fifty-two feet long, diagonally built on oak frames with a raking bow; there was a wheel-box amidships and a funnel. The first thing to come off was the smoke-stack! I can't abide chimneys on a boat. I moved the wheel-box aft and shortened all the steering wires.

One Friday morning whilst taking my 'crocodile' to school, I spotted the vicar standing outside the porch to St. George's Church, wringing his hands and looking most upset. The previous evening we had had a gale which had blown down a big pine tree across the gateway to the church. "And how, Mr. North, am I going to get my congregation into the building? I'll never get any one to shift it before Sunday." Big-hearted Northy - I offered to move it for him! With some of the senior boys I sawed it into ten foot lengths (the branches kept us in firewood all winter!) and I cut out a lovely big crook, which I later used as a 'fiddle' for the bow of my boat, and carved it into the figurehead of a mermaid. The ten-foot lengths I sawed into planking. I used the lot. I picked up thirty oak stanchions and bolted them aft round the stern of *Michaela*.

Lying in the mud at Southampton was an old Yankee schooner and for five pounds I bought the poop-rail - it was about five inches by three inches of lovely teak. Scraped and varnished it shone like silk. I joined it onto my stanchions and on each end I carved a dolphin. She was beginning to take shape!

The old trading schooner *Lady of Avenel* was lying in the mud in Holes Bay, Poole. She had settled on her own anchor during the war, remaining there ever since. I nipped on board in my gumboots one evening and came away with a bagful of dead-eyes which I used on *Michaela*. For power I used a fifty-horsepower Paxman diesel (which had at one time turned a Navy generator), buttoned it up to the existing shaft and fitted a smaller propeller. A pair of fishing-boat masts were stepped on deck in tabernacles with the shortest at the back so she turned out to be a ketch (schooner?). For the saloon I bought the oak panelling (out of a tailor's dressing-room when it was being enlarged) for three pounds. The steering-wheel I found on the beach in Normandy during the war - it had hung on the wall ever since as a souvenir. I even crossed a yard on the fore-mast and fitted Jack-yard topsails. It was a lot of work of course but I enjoyed doing it.

We were having a drink one evening at the 'Saxon King', our local pub, not far from Hengistbury Head, and during the conversation one of our neighbours mentioned that for their holiday they had been to the Costa Brava.

"Never heard of it," I said. "Where is it?"

"It has just been found," she said.

Spain was now evidently the 'in' place for holidays and the exchange rate was fantastic. That summer, having no boat to sail, we took the plane to Barcelona and explored Catalunia by bus and rail. We had a couple of sleeping-bags and stayed in hostels and small hotels each night. There were few enough foreigners about in those days. We hadn't a word of Spanish but the people were charming and we vowed that if we ever got a car (and learned to drive!) that we would go again, and in the meantime try to learn a bit of the language. It was at Ondarra that we saw our first bullfight. A fiesta. Any aficionado who reads this may be interested to know we saw Julio Aparicio, Antonio Bienvenida, Juan Garcia 'Mondeno', Gregorio Sanchez, Miguel Baez Litri, Duque and the long-retired *rejoneador*, Duque de Piñohermosa. We cut fourteen ears, three tails and 'Mondeno' cut a hoof. I loved it, and Sylvia, a confirmed animal lover, was fascinated.

We promptly bought *The Swords of Spain* by Robert Daly, and *Aficionado* by Keyhoe, and sat on the beach and started to mug up *los toros*. When we asked the proprietor of the hotel if there would be another fight that week, he said, "Señor, Señora, if, as you say, you saw the performance in Ondarra today - please - never again go to a bullfight! You have seen the best! You will never see another like it again!" And, on reflection, I don't think we ever have.

Time went on and *Michaela* was just about completed. I had been a so-called housemaster for years - I got on well with the boys, but my feet were starting to itch.

"Sylvia," I said one day, looking very innocent. "If we took *Michaela* down to the Med - to Spain, we could charter her and see a bullfight every Sunday."

"What about the school? The business is just starting to pay off!"

"Yes, I know, but I feel like a spare part. I can't do this for the rest of my life! Anyway, think about it."

"Heigh-ho!" said Sylvia. "Off we go again! I can see that for the rest of my life I'm going to metaphorically pick up my kit-bag and follow you. We shan't have any money, you know."

"Why do we want money? I know it comes in very useful but living is far more important! Money can buy a lot of pleasure but it can't buy happiness!"

Chapter 31

One of the teachers at the school decided he wanted to run the business. He was a very nice, plump, pompous little man and rather fancied himself as an ecclesiastic. When he took over the boarding school the first thing he did was to convert the garage into a chapel, much to the disgust of the senior boys.

We then lived on the boat for a month or two, during which time we were adopted by a young terrier who for some reason only answered to the name of Scrappie. She came over the gangplank one morning, sniffed around, inspected us and decided, "Yes, this will do," - and settled down! A few weeks later she delivered four puppies - much to Sylvia's delight, and from then on, daily, we were fishing pups out of the bilges, rescuing them from the river, and pulling them out from under the fly-wheel. Sylvia swore the dog was a Llasso Apso - must have read it in a book somewhere - she looked more like a fox-terrier gone wrong to me! She was a very intelligent little dog, however, and we came to love her dearly. Nobody could get within twenty yards of her boat without getting barked at. We pushed off one day, vaguely intending to go down westward. We didn't get very far, as it happened, halfway across the bay it was decided for no particular reason to go into Poole. Coming alongside the quay I threw a rope to a bearded young chap who made it fast to a bollard.

"Where was she built," he said, "Denmark?"

"No."

"She is a Scowegian?"

"No."

"She's not a little fruit-boat from the West Indies?"

"No."

"Come on," he said, "where is she from?"

"Come on board and have a beer and I'll tell ya! But first have a look at the quarter badges on her stern."

"Christ!" he said, "she's ex-Royal Navy!"

His name was Noel Tringham, a Welshman. He was bosun on an M.L. moored out in the harbour converted for use as a floating sailing school. Boating was beginning to boom and sailing outfits were starting up all around the coast.

"Why don't you come out and tie up alongside," he said. "Our guests would love to look over her - she's a fantastic conversion - and I'll give you a beer from our bar on board. Well, what about it?"

I would go anywhere for a free beer so off we went. Tying up alongside *Rozita* we met the owner, a practising doctor, and were duly presented with a drink. We were introduced to his guests and they all piled on board my boat, much to Scrappie's disgust. They popped up and down the hatch and scrambled up the rigging having a high old time. Nothing happened for half an hour and the people were either reading or talking quietly amongst themselves or looking out of the windows. There was no 'personality' on board at all. It was obvious, when they had done their stint of sailing they had to look after themselves. I leaned over to Sylvia -

"This is as dead as mutton, mate," I said. "Let's get the place going."

She grinned. "It is a bit dull - what are we going to sing first? *The Dirty Old Woman Who Lived in Pall-Mall* or *Eskimo Nell*?"

"Give over," I said. But within twenty minutes they were all laughing and talking and buying drinks as fast as the owner could dish them out. One of them fetched up a guitar - he'd never been asked before. They started singing like birds! The owner looked most impressed - this is what he had envisaged but it had never happened.

"Where are you two going from here?" asked the owner-doctor.

"Well now, we had thought of going down to the Med and doing a bit of chartering - or something."

"How about joining us and running this outfit! You seem to be able to organise a crowd of odd bods and to get them going. You know what I mean."

"Yes, I know what you mean, but the Med does sound rather attractive."

"Well, look. Suppose you both join us for a year, and if it's a success you could go down to the Med and start up a pilot scheme down there."

I gave my wife a querying look. Sylvia, who had been sitting with a blank expression on her face suddenly burst into a fit of giggles.

"My word, Northy," she said, "you hop around so much I can't keep up with you! I don't mind what we do - we could stay here for another year and then go down to Spain, at least we should have a bit more money behind us."

"Well," I said, "were we to take this on, there are one or two changes I should want to make."

"Such as?"

I grinned apologetically. "In the first place, you are in the wrong harbour. You sit out here a mile offshore, sandbanks all around you - with wind against tide your guests spend more time in the water than in their dinghies. If it's raining they get soaking wet before they get ashore in that old cutter - and that's one man's job keeping that serviced, I'll bet!"

He nodded. "I hadn't thought about that," he said. "Where would you go?"

"Dartmouth," I said promptly. "Miles of sheltered

harbour and you could get a mooring a couple of hundred yards from the shore - lovely beaches, nearby railway station laid on, and it's a very pretty little town."

A couple of days later we sailed down to Dartmouth in *Michaela*. Sylvia had never seen the town before and immediately fell in love with it. It had not yet been 'found'. Cottage properties could be bought for a few hundred pounds. There was a lovely big four-bedroomed villa overlooking the river offered to us for two thousand pounds. Every third house was for sale. I say this because, out of curiosity, I had spoken to a house-agent with the idea of getting a store ashore for 'Sail-a-Boat Holiday', should they decide to come down there. Picking up a *Countryman* magazine we saw an advertisement, 'For Sale Kingwear Castle with fifteen acres of rough land, 3,500 pounds'. Dartmouth Castle and Kingwear Castle in ancient times were linked by a chain-boom to keep out pirates. We sailed along to Blackpool Sands, rowed ashore and had a picnic, then back up the River Dart to Totnes. Sylvia loved it! "I think I would rather live here than go to the Med," she enthused. "Trees, trees, everywhere we look - in the spring it must be lovely. Let's live here, shall we?"

"If you wish, my old dear - but they don't have many bullfights!"

Rozita was turned around in the autumn and moored over on the Kingwear side of the channel and we accepted the job of running 'Sail-a-Boat Holiday'. A store and workshop were obtained on the quayside and the dinghies were brought ashore for painting and overhaul. We lived in *Michaela* during the winter whilst the base-ship was given a coat of paint. There was a big Aga cooker on board and Sylvia reorganised the galley. In the springtime we roamed the banks of the Dart and gathered primroses and wild daffodils. I'd never seen my girl so happy! Even Scrappie approved. I designed a 'Sailafloat' brochure and the local tradespeople put in adverts which helped to pay for it.

The following Easter season started with a full complement of guests - the owner was delighted. The townspeople accepted Sylvia at once, me they were not too sure about. One old gaffer was boasting to me over a drink one night that he'd lived there all his life and never been farther than Torquay! What about that then? He beamed with pride at the thought of it! "What do you want for that then, a bloody medal?" I said. He looked aghast at my lack of fervent admiration, saying, "I'm a Dartmouthian".

Putting a rig on the old thirty-foot cutter we could tow half a dozen dinghies out of the entrance and round to Castle Cove for swimming and sailing. The local townspeople were delighted to be invited on board for one of our parties, Sylvia would pick the prettiest girl-guest to be barmaid for the evening and sales of drinks sky-rocketed. We engaged another sailing instructor and a couple of students to help out in the summer. The following winter we had a stand at the Boat Show on the east coast, and the result was very satisfying. Our two boys came down to Dartmouth when they got the opportunity, they were both very good small-boatmen and helped us a lot. Michael North went to the Merchant Navy - Michael Harding to the Royal Navy.

Chapter 32

Two more seasons passed very happily. Then the owner, for domestic reasons, decided to sell the business. We hadn't enough money to buy it ourselves, but I did show around various would-be purchasers. It was eventually bought by an ex-R.N.R. Lt. Commander.

On the river opposite our mooring was the local gasworks. Unused for years, the gasometer was working only as a storage tank for the town. The property was surrounded by a twenty-foot high stone wall. Behind it was a clutter of rusty sheds, pump-rooms, coke heaps and a brick chimney about two hundred feet high. It was only about forty feet across the road to the river where coal barges used to lie. We had discussed the idea before, what a wonderful position for a sailing hotel! Self-catering holidays were becoming popular in Spain - why not here! I had an offer for *Michaela* - we'd only ever used her for quick trips up and down the coast, so although it was a bit of a wrench, we took the offer.

Sylvia, being the businesswoman put on her smartest outfit and went to Plymouth to interview the Regional Manager of the Gas Company and came back beaming. They wanted to get rid of the property and said they'd help as much as they could. Of course it had just been nationalized and money was no object. I drew out rough plans of what we envisaged and Sylvia visited all the Devon banks to see if they would back us with a loan. It all seemed rather scary. At that time 80% would be advanced on a run-down hotel.

But self-catering was unheard of in the U.K. Spain had jumped ahead on this and we had seen it working - and, well! Sailing was a nebulous thing - wouldn't we rather build an ordinary hotel. Sailing oh - Head Office wouldn't like that. Eventually the manager of Martin's Bank in Torquay made an appointment to view the gasworks. When he arrived it was pouring with rain and the property looked awful! Anyway, climbing over a pile of very rusty ironwork, he and Sylvia stood on top of the wall under an umbrella whilst she enthused over the view, the river, the future etc. and by the time they got down he had agreed to a loan. Good old Mrs. North - she could sell ice-cream to an Eskimo!

We borrowed thousands and thousands of pounds at four and a half percent interest. The thought of it had frightened me to death. Of course before the ink was dry it went up to five and a half, then six and a half, then seven and a half, then your friend and mine, Harold Wilson was enthroned and it went up to nine, ten, eleven percent before we had finished building the place. Anyway, she had got the brass! Plans were drawn and approved by the local council, then we started demolishing the buildings behind the wall. I personally knocked down the big twenty-foot chimney - and I got a lot of satisfaction out of doing that! You should try it some time - by yourself. Buy yourself a chimney and knock it down! The old foreman's cottage at the back of the yard was reconditioned first of all, and we moved in (with the Delft), one room becoming an office for Sylvia.

Then we had to think of a name. Something new, something boaty, and Sylvia immediately thought up the name, Boatel.

"That's a silly name," I said, with a little sneer, but I couldn't at the moment think of a better one.

"Why is it silly? We've had motels for years - why not a boatel?"

Why not? It was a very good clear word, as it turned out,

so much so that an American firm saw it in the English newspapers and decided to build a similar outfit backing on 42nd Street, New York and to call it a Boatel. With all the cheek in the world Sylvia, knowing that only goods could be trademarked and bluffing hard, warned the New York firm against the use of the word Boatel which she had coined and would give to the nation in ten years. But until that time - it was not for world use. The New Yorkers withdrew (and invited us to visit). We held the name for ten years until with the tremendous growth of the sport of sailing it became a household word, which brought a lot of publicity. And my old lady thought of it! I said she was clever.

The idea of the Boatel was to have a number of self-catering flatlets designed to sleep four persons, each compact and simple with a galley kitchenette off the lounge. There were bars on the ground floor and a restaurant to be used for the evening meals. Families could holiday cheaply and in comfort - Mum and the girls watch Dad and the eldest son sailing on the river down below through the huge picture-windows. 'Bring your own boat or use ours. Instruction if desired. Use of workshop and parking for cars and trailers.' We bought an old floating-bridge from the Dartmouth Ferry Co. After cutting off the useless ironwork, with lifting-ramps at each end, it was ideal for pulling out our Enterprise dinghies. With fenders all around, it made a very convenient mooring for learner sailors to use. As soon as we had knocked down the old stone wall (using the material for in-filling) I painted a huge sign about thirty feet long with a painting of the proposed building and all the information about the Boatel.

Around that time the B.B.C. started a programme entitled *The Get-Ahead Competition*, sponsored by the *News Chronicle*. Anyone with a bright idea and lacking finance could enter and put their scheme before a panel of judges - a businessman, an M.P., a trade union leader, Stanley

Matthews, and Baroness Wootten - a social economist. Twelve thousand people entered, their ideas were sifted through each week, four people were picked to put them forward to the panel - the winner then going ahead to the next heat. There was a special section for ladies, and thirty-five hundred entries were put forward. Sylvia again, as the Brains Department, was prodded into entering - pushed would be a better word - and, believe it or not, ended up in the final with three other ladies. Of course the *News Chronicle* was delighted with our idea of a Boatel - they had also sponsored the building of the Enterprise dinghy, of which we had ten. The final programme was introduced by Peter West (according to Sylvia, he was more nervous than she was). However, Baroness Wootten said that, as we had formed a private company the week before the final programme, any monies obtained would go to the company - and not to Sylvia as an individual, which, of course, was reasonably correct. On the strength of that a lady who had a new idea for breeding pigs won first place and Sylvia was allowed to come second. This was rather disappointing (for the *News Chronicle* too) but our accountant reckoned we must have had twenty-five thousand pounds' worth of free advertising as all the national newspapers picked it up, and we eventually had letters from all over the world congratulating us on the idea.

The day the Boatel opened we were still finishing off painting. I was standing in the foyer dressed in an old pair of jeans and a battered peaked cap. There was the sound of squealing brakes outside the door. A rather smart gentleman dressed in blazer, grey slacks, sailing shoes and regimental tie jumped out of an Aston Martin, behind which was a trailer holding a spanking new twelve foot dinghy. Oops, our first guest! I opened the door as he nipped smartly up the steps -

"Good morning," he said, "I'm afraid I'm rather early. My name is Norman Sargent. I do have a booking - is the manager around? What!"

Smiling a big toothy smile, I said, "As a matter of fact, we don't have a manager, but I'm one of the directors." I thought fast, "And that's a cracking little dinghy you have there." (Tell them what they want to know - Dale Carnegie on *How to Win Friends and Influence People*.)

"You think so?" he said, looking at it affectionately. "I love it but I can't sail the bloody thing."

"Tell you what, Norman - by the way, my name is Frank - if I can't get you to sail around those three buoys (pointing them out) in three hours flat - I'll buy you a bottle of whisky!"

"No! Really old chap? Fantastic! When can we start?"

"As soon as you get her rigged. I'll send one of the boys to give you a hand."

"Right!" he said, turning to go up the stairs, his room key in hand.

"Norman," I chipped in, "will you take this tin of paint up to the lad on the next floor. His name is Ken - he's got more medals for sailing than I've had good dinners!"

"Delighted," he said. "I'll give you a hand, painting, later if you like." He trotted upstairs with the tin of paint in one hand and a very small suitcase in the other.

Click, click, I thought. This is what he wants! He wants to be one of the lads. He doesn't want a lot of formality. He gets that fifty weeks a year! (We found out later that he was the Parliamentary secretary to M.P. Gerald Nabarro. Knowing nothing about the hotel business we worked on that hunch.) We were known as Sylvia and Frank to everyone in Dartmouth and all who came to stay with us at the Boatel. The staff were known by their Christian names. It was most informal but it worked - it wouldn't have done for the Governor but we didn't have that sort of clients. We managed to get a Club licence (an open licence used by pubs in those days was an impossibility!) It was the first club as such in Dartmouth. The local businesspeople joined, the staff of the R.N. College, plus the lads, crews of Naval vessels and visiting yachtsmen. We held a dance every Friday and specials for Valentine's Eve, Bonfire Night, Christmas and New Year's Eve when all were expected to come in fancy dress.

The following year we again had a stand at the Boat Show at Earl's Court where we did quite a lot of business and met lots of our last season's clients (for whom we kept the odd bottle of whisky under the table). For the back of the stand I had painted a mural of Dartmouth harbour and I had carved a rather voluptuous figurehead as a 'stopper' (when anyone stopped and gaped we popped in a brochure). It looked good over the boatshed doors in Dartmouth afterwards. Later in the year I received a letter from a Com. Hemworth asking if it was for sale. Naturally I said yes, and, on receiving his cheque, sent the carving as requested to the next Boat Show. I took a couple of our girls (staff) with me to help on the stand, and walking around the show espied on the Hemworth Boat and Caravan Stand my old figurehead!

"Look!" said one of the lasses. "There's your figurehead - let's go and talk to the man."

"No - I shouldn't bother him," I said.

"But yes!" said the girl. She trotted over and was given its full history.

"It came off a schooner called *Queen of the Islands*, wrecked on such-and-such an atoll in 1884."

So what do you know! "Well," I thought, "he's happy with it. The girls are happy. I'm very happy." So, if you do know of anyone who wants an antique figurehead ...

That winter we were approached by someone who wanted to join us as a working director so, on the strength of that we opened another Boatel in Cawsands Bay. We bought a big old house on the beach with fish-cellars below and, when it was converted, we had six flatlets, six double-bunk cabins and about five Enterprise dinghies. The cellars were made into a bar-cum-dining room, the bar itself being exactly six feet six inches in width. The place must have been three or four hundred years old, the walls built onto the beach were six feet thick and made of solid stone. With an easterly wind the waves broke against the house, spray flying over the roof, leaving seaweed on the telephone wires behind it. Some of the old beams had to be cut out for conversion to a Boatel; these I carved and built into the bar. Again we managed to get a Club licence - the local L.V.A. fought hard against it and a rather hard-nosed old gentleman objected to our singing and 'funny' dancing, to which the Chief Magistrate exclaimed - "Mr. So-and-so, you really must keep up with the times - this is the new dance and it's called the Twist. Please get a chair for Mrs. North - she is having to stand here for hours answering rather unimportant questions." Sylvia had spoken to the young policeman on duty on the quay a couple of evenings previously and asked if we were making too much noise. "Not to worry, me lovely," he had said, "these old gaffers will complain wotever you do - I don't think you are making much noise or I'd tell you." And on the strength of that remark the court had to wait while he was brought from North Devon to confirm this, which he did - and we got our licence.

I moved down to run the Plymouth Sound Boatel and the new director took over at Dartmouth to help Sylvia. The Cawsands Boatel also went like a bomb from the word go! The village people joined and local fishermen and dockyard mateys could be found at the bar drinking with pretty girls in bikinis. Two stone steps led down behind the bar, and as I was rather stuck for space, I was tapping around there with a hammer one day when I hit a loose stone. Chiselling it out I found another cellar down below. Obviously it had been a smugglers' 'hide' at some time. All I found in there was a Napoleonic French bayonet, but the space made a fine beer-cellar, as it was below high-water mark and was always very cool.

For three hundred pounds I bought an old converted thirty-foot Mevagissey pilchard-boat with a pet/paraffin engine and rigged with second-hand lifeboat sails. It was very popular with our guests, most of whom came from inland towns and had never sailed in anything bigger than a dinghy. Occasionally we would take it around to the Plymouth Sailing School - known by the young naval gentlemen as the 'Groin Exchange'.

One of our club members happened to mention to me over the bar that he was going to knock down an old cottage in Millbrook, a village a couple of miles away. He couldn't sell it so he intended to build a bungalow on the land. We nipped over to have a look. It was delightful, very shabby, of course, but built of stone it had a small garden with an arched gateway. The roof was tiled with hand-cut slates, varying in size from the size of a playing card at the ridge to heavy thirty inch slates at the gutter, fastened with wooden pegs. There was a strange carved window in the kitchen which later I found out to be one of the old stern windows of the wooden *Foudroyant*. We bought the cottage for the price he'd paid on the land and used it as a getaway place when Sylvia came over to check the accounts.

Oh, then we bought a horse! He was a cross-Exmoor pony of about fifteen hands called Trica - I called him Treacle but he didn't seem to mind. Anyway, we were both stuck on him. He was owned by an old farmer who used him for his milk-round and had treated the poor animal abominably. The farmer would get very drunk then lash the poor old brute up the road, with milk-cans rattling and banging until the poor old pony was scared to death.

"You're agoin' to 'ave an accident on' o' these days, Fred," he was warned. "That's no way to treat a horse." It happened, of course. The old boy fell out of the trap and broke his leg. Treacle was put into a leaky old shed and left in the dark. The farmer seemed to be scared to death of him and wouldn't even open the door to clean out the muck. The horse was thrown a bundle of hay and given an occasional bucket of water. He was knee-deep in cack - the place stank! We heard about this and went up to see the old farmer. "Eighty quid I wants fer 'im," he said. "Tek it or leave it!" Against everyone's advice we took it. We went up to see Treacle the following day. Opening the stable doors he started to flatten his ears, roll his eyes and back up into the darkest corner. Sylvia said, "Come on in and talk to him, he's frightened."

"Not bloody likely," I said, "I'm more frightened than he is!"

She went up, blew up his nose and talked horse-talk to him. His ears came forward and she gently rubbed his head. "Come on, old fellow, let's go out in the sunshine."

He stopped quivering. We looked him over, stroked him and examined our purchase. His hooves were soft and had spread from living in the slush. His coat had matted where he had rolled in the filthy stable. Talking gently to him all the time we took him down the road, put him in a comfortable stall with the door open and plenty of dry straw and fresh hay. Sylvia loved him and talked about him for hours. We walked him for miles, cut his hooves and painted them with Stockholm Tar. He gradually came back to life. We bought some second-hand tack and walked and trotted him around a paddock we had hired until one day he broke into a canter and we reckoned we had won. We bought horse books and read about snaffles and fetlocks, and I was warned never again to call his halter a headrope - it just wasn't done in riding circles. I still have a book entitled *Elements of Hunting* and I got a huntin' pink weskit from Gieves. When I wore it years later for Christmas the real horsey people - the ones who go around poking pigs with sticks on Sunday mornings, didn't really mind when I climbed up on the horse and said "let go for'ard - let 'er go aft," but the bit of rope in front had to be called a halter - definitely *not* - *not* a painter! - And one mounts a horse, one doesn't go topside. Sylvia bought me a pair of jodhpurs for Christmas and I was told that I should wear a 'funny 'at'. "No, but I could wear the steel helmet I wore during the war." They said, "Sorry, but it's really not done - only military gentlemen from the Brigade of Guards wore tin-hats when riding to hounds. Royalty have been black-balled by the Queen even for wearing a motor-cycle crash helmet. Arthur Scargill could wear a miner's helmet - willy-nilly - but in that case it was called a Militant Tendency.

Sylvia would go up to Trica's paddock with a book, sit near him and read. He would slowly sidle up and then lie down alongside. If she lay down - he would sit up and keep his eyes open, looking around. When she sat up he would lie down. Very curious! We mentioned this to an old cavalry man who pooh-poohed the idea, until one afternoon he came up and watched over the gate. He went away scratching his head - dumbfounded! Treacle taught us both to ride. Thump his ribs as much as we could - he just wouldn't gallop until he thought we were ready - after that either one of us could gallop happily all afternoon.

When we closed the Cawsands Boatel at the end of the season, Treacle came back with us in a trailer and we hired grazing at Dartmouth for the winter. Scrappie would bark to be taken up on the saddle - she was getting a bit too long in the tooth now for a lot of exercise. One Sunday morning I had been for a ride and was walking him to the paddock holding his new halter when we met Sylvia coming from the church, dressed in a smart black costume with a saucy little hat perched on her head. She had gone blonde by this time and did look rather nice.

"Hello, love," she said. "Hello, me old horse!" She blew up his nose and scratched his ears. We were alongside the recreation ground. "Give me a bunk up and tie t'other end of the halter to his nose - I'm going to have a short, sharp gallop." She hiked up her tight skirt and slid over his bare back.

"You're showing your knickers - you saucy old woman," said I.

"Treek doesn't mind, do you pet?" She kicked off her high-heeled shoes, thumped him with her stockinged feet and was away across the rugby pitch, mud flying from the horse's hooves. She hadn't gone thirty yards when I heard her squeal - she lost the halter and clung to his neck - her hat went flying, t'owd pony thought it was part of a game, and increased his stride. Round the field they went, turned at the end and galloped up towards me. I held my arms open and Treacle slowed down and stopped in front of me, blowing hard and I just caught Sylvia as she slipped off his back.

"What happened, mate?" I grinned. "Going in for circus stuff, are you?"

"Gawd!" she said, "I was so frightened. I forgot I had on nylon stockings and things - I couldn't get a grip with my legs - I was slipping off all the time! And you are eating too much, Treek - you're getting as fat as a pig!" - She stroked his nose and gave him a kiss.

Coming back in the Mini to Dartmouth one afternoon from Plymouth, I was slowed down by a motorcycle cop who waved me into a gateway. Anyone who knows that part of Devon will bear me out - the roads are so narrow and the banks are so high that they really are tunnels without tops. As I cut the engine a big open touring car came slowly around the bend with a tall gentleman standing up in the back. I know that face, I thought, and as he passed I waved and said, "Hello there!" He waved back. "Sorry to trouble you, old chap!" he shouted, and it wasn't until I started the engine and set off again I remembered the face. It was Prince Philip! Unknown to me, the Royal Yacht had entered the harbour and made fast whilst H.R.H. had nipped ashore to keep an appointment in Exeter. When I got back to Dartmouth Sylvia was all agog.

"I said hello to Prince Philip, and he waved to me!" she exclaimed.

"How did that happen?" I said.

"Well, I was standing on the flat roof of the Boatel looking at the Royal Yacht Britannia through binoculars and I spotted the Prince looking at the Boatel through his glasses. I waved and automatically I said 'Hello' and he waved back and said 'Hello' too. What about that!"

One could hardly call it hob-nobbing, but we have both spoken to a member of the Royal Family!

In 1962 the Tall Ships Race started from Dartmouth. What a fantastic sight that was! Wind-jammers of all nations tied up, bow to stern, the whole length of the harbour. We were very happy to be invited for cocktails on board the huge Italian *Vespucci*. For days poor old Sylvia never left her desk, making out temporary membership cards for all the cadets who made a beeline for the boats. Each one had to be done carefully, as we had a rather rich, cantankerous, old gentleman living in the apartment next door who vowed he would get our licence taken away from us. He also paid spies to try and catch us out at closing times. He became such a pain-in-the-ass eventually, that we briefed Counsel to stop him. He beat us in the end, however. He died the evening before the case came up in court.

One Saturday a rather nice old cruiser tied up to one of our buoys and the skipper rowed ashore asking if he may stay there just for the night. Naturally, I said yes he could, and over a beer he told us that he was on a delivery job, the owner having died whilst the yacht was in Belle Isle. "I think he was quite a well-known person," said the skipper. "His name was Osborne - Don or Dod - something like that." Well, well! Old Dod! I raised my tankard and drank a silent toast to the amiable old rascal. Bet he's up there now, blinding them all with his science.

One evening, over the bar, a friend of mine rather sadly told me he was going to break up his old yacht, *Elaine*, to get the lead off her keel as no one wanted to buy her. He showed me her photograph, thirty-two feet of a six foot six inch beam and four foot six inch draught. Six foot six inch beam? Built in 1906? Cotton rigged with a long bowsprit and deep cockpit? Her underwater sections were lovely but I could see she was hogged. Hogged! What an awful word to a sailing man. All boats built in her day had a sweet curve fore and aft, the bow being slightly higher than the stern. This one was flat, and if anything, her stern was slightly down. She was hogged! I was talking about this a couple of days later to Cawsands' Arthur Dawe - one of the finest shipwrights I have ever known.

"Where's she be lying, me 'andsome?"

I told him. "Up the river Tamar."

"Well," he said. "Whyn't we go up an' 'ave a look at 'er?"

We did. He crawled inside her, tapped, prodded, and muttered to himself.

"How much did 'ee say 'ee wanted fer 'er?"

"The value of the lead on her keel - about two hundred or two hundred and fifty pounds, I should think."

"Well, you can't go far wrong there, me old mate - she'd cost a fortune to build now with that timber in 'er. She'd mek a pretty li'l boat, Oi racken! Bit of work to do on 'er mind you!"

"But she's hogged!"

"Oh, she's a bit 'ogged, but we can cure that. If you wants to sail 'er - buy 'er!"

I did and had her towed round to Millbrook Creek. Arthur carefully took out all the copper nails in her stringers and the planking aft, and, as we worked and 'plonked', her hull gradually came back into shape. With the narrow beam and deep keel it was very difficult to work inside, but he fitted new frames and three watertight bulkheads. Raising the deck aft of the cockpit and building up the transom gave me a small sleeping cabin instead of the useless overhang, and also stiffened up the stern. I cut up a perfectly good mahogany table for the transom itself, carved on it mermaids and fishes and her name *Elaine of Dartmouth*, and then gilded it with ex-G.P.O. gold leaf. We made a new mast and rigged her as a ketch-cum-schooner with a gaff-sail on the foremast and a rung on the peal running through a small block on the main-mast. The jib was a big one fixed on a roller so she would sail under various combinations of rig. I glass-fibred the boat up to the boot-topping, the hull was dark green with a mahogany topstrake and had a suit of ochre red nylon sails. The bow was fitted with a small fiddle, holding a gilded mermaid figurehead and the break to the poopdeck terminated with carved and gilded dolphins. A ten foot ash sweep was carried in the shrouds and fitted into a rowlock on top of the transom and used as a yolah; it was very useful for trundling about the moorings. Everything I had ever learned I put to use. Finding it difficult climbing up the mast with a damaged back, I fixed ratlines on the foremast or small canvas steps on the main. Self-steering was fitted on the rudder-head. I fitted roller-reefing, but in practice found it easier to drop a sail and/or shorten the jib, until in strong winds with four and a half tons of head she would, on her keel, bowl along nicely with just her little gaff foresail. She would sail like a witch. The cockpit was fitted with a zipped canvas cover - I could sit in my tiny doghouse as dry as a bone with a hosepipe playing on it (I tried it once!). The power unit was a six-horsepower air-cooled diesel with a reversing prop - I doubt if it was used more than half a dozen times as I made it a 'thing' to sail up to my moorings at any state of the tide - well, we had to in the old *Two Brothers* - we didn't have an engine. I was rather taken aback one day, however, when a brass-bound yachtsman in a beautiful Gieves blazer accused me of doing it to show off! But that little boat hauled like a dinghy. I loved her - if she had been a wee bit smaller I would have put her in a bottle on the mantelpiece. She took nearly three years to finish, and I longed for the day when I would sail her single-handed to Greece.

One afternoon a tall young man came into the bar as we were closing. "Hello, Peter," I said, "nice to see you again." We had taught him to sail the previous summer. "How are you?"

"Fine - I've got my own boat now. Oh, this is Charles, a friend of mine."

"How are you?"

"Watneys, if I remember rightly? Yes?" I drew a couple of pints of ale. "Bring them over to the cottage, lads - it's after time and as you know we still have a nasty neighbour." The three of us walked across the yard and into the little house at the back. We sat by the log-fire talking boats. Charles, looking around the room espied my old tatty sword leaning against the corner.

"That's one of our swords, surely?" he said.

"What do you mean, one of yours? It's mine - it's a Navy sword."

"I can see that," he said smiling. "I'm sorry - but my name is Wilkinson."

"You make razor blades then?"

He grinned - "Frank, if you like I'll send it home and get it refurbished."

And he did. It still looks smashing.

Chapter 33

It was the end of the holiday season when the B.B.C. appeared on our doorstep. Film producer Peter Graham Scott and John Fabian, the director, asked if we could accommodate about forty members of his television company for two or three weeks. We were delighted, of course, as it meant a lot of business just when we needed it. Our summer staff had finished - most of them had gone back to university, so when we were told that a big, cooked, early breakfast (5:30 a.m.) would be required for all, Sylvia took on the job herself. Otherwise either chef would draw double pay.

"Frank," said Peter. "I bet you don't know of an old topsail schooner we could charter?"

"Bet I do!" I said. "My friend, Jim McGreth, has got one - hang on a minute and I'll give him a ring."

That was the start of the famous B.B.C. serial *The Onedin Line*. Jim was a retired B.E.A. senior pilot, a fantastic navigator, but with little knowledge of sailing. He had always wanted a boat, however, and thought he might as well have a big one whilst he was at it, so he went over to Denmark and bought this old topsail schooner.

Charlotte was built about 1904 with the usual fore and aft rig and big square fore-topsail. She'd had installed a very ancient single-cylinder engine, no gearbox, merely a reversing propeller. When entering harbour, a hand stood below decks holding a big rusty iron lever. One bang on the deck with a hammer meant ahead, two bangs meant astern, and three bangs meant neutral. This last was a bit difficult as neutral was neither one thing nor t'other and one had to put one's foot on the propshaft to see which way she was going. It would be rather tricky in a bit of a seaway. The owner was delighted with the idea of a long charter, which would help to pay for the new sails and eventually towards a new engine. She was moored against the sea-wall outside the Boatel where she dried out at low water, and all hands went overside to scrub and anti-foul her bottom. Dartmouth, of course, was an ideal location for a nineteenth-century film, with its old gabled houses and narrow cobbled streets. The castles at the harbour entrance, the steep wooded banks, and the lovely Dart itself winding inland for miles up to Totnes, were such suitable locations for that type of film. The *Mayflower* herself set sail from Dartmouth Quay in 1620, but owing to leaky water-barrels had to turn back to Plymouth. Had that not happened, the *Mayflower*'s passengers to this day would have been called the Dartmouth Brethren.

All the extras in the film were local people and 'Australian Jim' and I the sailing masters and from that day forth the skipper was known as Mac. It was all great fun and I got a tremendous thrill out of steering this old schooner with everything drawing, a cloud of spray flying over her bows - she was a lot bigger than *Half-Pint*. Many of the actors had never been afloat before so it was a great experience for them, of course, and they were a lovely crowd of people to work with. Peter Gilmore as James Onedin was a grand person, full of fun, and his film wife was a real charmer. Mr. Baines, the Mate (Howard Lang ex-R.N.V.R.) knew more dirty rugby songs than I did. We had a very good party one evening which kept all the youngest members amused as we reminisced with a series of Do you remember this one? Cyril Abrahams who wrote *The Onedin Line* was an ex-Merchant Seaman, ex-miner, and ex-bus driver, and he always managed to get a bit part in every episode. He completely confounded the critics who decided after the first of the series that it just wouldn't make a serial. As it happened the programme was sold to forty countries, twice nominated for an award by the Writers' Guild and has been translated into four languages. Videos are now made of *The Onedin Line*.

It was whilst doing my usual Boatel stint at the London Boat Show that I met Chay Blythe who together with another man had rowed across the Atlantic just to see if they could do it. Now, of course, it's done by Americans who want to get their names in the Guinness Book of Records. (About the time of writing, the latest boat is about ten feet six inches - give or take an inch or two - and they sail downhill - from west to east. And the best of U.S. luck to them!) Many of the Boat Show stand-holders, at the weekend, motor up to London, but, as I had a 'stand in' for the next few days, I decided to go back up North - I hadn't been there for twenty-five years.

I branched off at Preston and made my way to Blackpool, where I booked into a hotel on the front. It was February and very cold. There was half-a-gale blowing and the seas were breaking and throwing spray twenty feet high over the promenade. Where to go? I went into the Tower Ballroom. It was O.A.P. night and a few elderly people were doing a Valeta. Wandering out again I walked aimlessly up a darkened street. There was a swank electric sign 'Paradise Club'. I turned and walked up a flight of carpeted stairs. Another sign pointed upwards - this flight had no carpet, only lino. Another sign - Excelsior - upwards. Not even lino on this lot. I came to a door with a cardboard notice, 'Paradise Club - Members Only' - it wasn't very good sign-writing either, I noticed. I knocked and a small panel flipped open.

"'Ello!" said a broad North Country voice.

"Hello."

"You a member?"

"No - just passing through."

"Oh - well - don't matter, eh? Come in! You don't look like a copper anyway."

There was a big bare room about forty feet across, a small bar tucked into one corner with a brassy blonde lady behind, polishing her fingernails, a tiny stage tucked away in the far corner upon which a rather plump girl was slowly wiggling her bare bottom to the strains of a scratchy tape. Oh, dear! Sex rearing its ugly head in the North of England! I turned to the bar and ordered a small whisky. There was a tap on my arm and I looked around, and then down. A pretty dark-haired little girl about eighteen years old was looking up at me.

"'Ello," she said with a bright smile.

"Hello, love," - I smiled back.

"Do you live 'ere then?"

"No," I replied, "just passing through."

"Oh."

Silence.

"Are you in business then?"

"Yes, er - I suppose I am."

"Oh," (pause), "I'm in business too."

"Are you?" I said, (pause) "I expect you would like a drink."

"Yes, please," she answered right quickly, "gin and tonic with ice."

I ordered.

Silence.

She nudged me with her elbows just below my waist - she couldn't have been much more than four feet ten inches high.

"Mister."

"Yes?"

"I'm on business 'now' you know."

"Are you?" I said, trying to look puzzled.

"Oh! You know!" She dug me with her elbow again. "Can we do business together, d'ya think?" She fluttered her eyelids hopefully.

"What?" I said. "A pretty young lass like you and an old gentleman like me? I don't think so."

"Oh yes, we could, mister," she said. "I'd climb on top and do all the work. 'Onest!"

That's what I'd call real North Country hospitality!

The following morning I decided to make my way over to the town of Bury when I suddenly remembered the date - twenty-first of February! Tomorrow was Sylvia's birthday! I slowed down, and spotting an Interflora sign, I pulled up outside the shop. The bell tinkled as I walked through the doorway. I was admiring the flowers when a voice behind me said, "Hello, love, can I help you?" Turning I saw a rather plump attractive lady.

"Good morning," I said. "I wonder if you could organize a dozen red roses to be sent tomorrow without fail to this address in Dartmouth, Devon," and I handed her my card.

"Oh yes," she said, "no trouble. Are you on holiday then?"

"No, not really. I've just come from Blackpool - I used to live there when I was a boy."

"Well, I used to live in bloody Blackpool when I was a lad," a loud voice interrupted from the next room, and a fat bald man walked in.

"Well, I'll be buggered!" he said. "Franky North, ain't you?"

"Er - yes - er I am - I - er." I'd never been to Bury before in my life!

"Well, you must remember me - John Illingworth - we were in Sea Scouts together."

"Of course!" I said. "I just wasn't expecting to see anyone I knew." Laughing heartily I stuck out my hand, he shook it and led me into a room behind. By the time he'd fished out a bottle and a couple of glasses, I'd got him! He was the young assistant Scout Master who had put up the thirty pounds to buy the *Lord Marmion*, but in those days he had been tall and slim with blonde curly hair. We talked for about an hour about old times, exchanged addresses and swore to keep in touch etc.

Continuing my journey I crossed the Backbone of England, dropping down the other side into Yorkshire, making my way to Wakefield. Stopping at the heath above the town, I looked down once again on the Merrie Cittie! Ugh! Dozens of mill chimneys, only some of them smoking now. Electric pylons marching down the slope and spreading in a maze and mixing with the pall of smoke which hung over the gas 'ouse. A train loaded with coal-trucks rattled over the bridge as I passed the railway station and turned left into Charlotte Street. Acres of old back-to-back houses had been torn down. There were piles of rubble everywhere.

"I'm glad we moved to Bournemouth when we did, Mum," I murmured, looking upwards.

Charlotte Street was still standing. I parked the Mini and walked across the road to the old plumbers' shop, Tosser, and rubbed some of the old dirt off the window. There they were - baths, washbasins, and toilets of different colours - they were always white when I worked there - chromium taps (they were white metal in my day) ball cocks and bathroom fittings. It was all rather dusty now. Old Tosser had been Joe's racing pigeon man - he would take the birds miles away on the train and at a set time toss them in the air to fly back home where Joe would be standing outside his pigeon-loft timing them in. It was also Tosser's job to clean the showroom daily, and by the look of it the old chap had been gone a long time. There was a tap on my shoulder. I turned around to face an old feller in a flat cap with a muffler tied around his neck.

"'Ow do!" he said.

"'Ow do, mate," I answered.

"You looking for summat?"

"Well - er, yes, I was wondering if old Joe Woodhead was still alive?"

"Ee, no lad. Joe passed on years ago."

"What about his son, Jim, is he about?"

"No - young Jim died sudden-like about four years ago. 'Eart attack or summat! - Very sudden - nice lad, Jim!"

"Well, what a pity. I've come three hundred miles and I hoped to see one of the family."

"Three 'undred miles? By Gowd! That's a long way! Th'd better come over to my place and 'ave a bit o' scrawn. Come on, Elsie."

Looking down I saw he had a little whippet on a piece of string. Elsie wagged her slender tail and we all crossed the street and turned down an alleyway.

"I live down this 'ere ginnel now t'pits workin' - used 'ave cottage on t'illtop but ar'm gettin' a bit past it now, so me and Annie moved our bits o' things into town so she could be near pictures. Very fond of pictures is our Annie - and Bingo! Bloomin' hell, she's Bingo-daft, my old woman!"

(Down a couple of stone steps - their edges rubbed with 'Donkey-stone' and into a semi-basement.)

"Annie, luv," said my host, "set another plate for dinner - I've got a young fellow 'ere wot's come three unnert miles to see old Joe Wood'ead." He turned to me. "Tha'll atter go a lot further now to see t'owd lad. By 'eck!" and he chortled. "Sit thissen down, lad. Elsie, get under, you owd bugger," and shoved the dog gently with his foot under the table. "She's a nice little bitch ar' Elsie - like me tho', gettin' a bit past it. Won me a bob or two in 'er time. Ain't you, lass?" and the whippet pushed her fine pointed nose up between his knees and looked at him adoringly.

Annie came in wiping the perspiration from her face with a tea towel. "'Ello, love," she said. She had rosy chubby cheeks and black twinkling eyes. "We'ers tha' come from then, lad?"

"'Ee's come from t'South of England, would you believe?" She plonked a Yorkshire pudding down in front of me, big enough to choke a horse. It was fat and crackly and full of gravy. In the North, Yorkshire pudding is served as a separate first course - the idea being, if you eat enough pud, you won't want so much meat. You've got to think of the brass. Roast beef, roast potatoes, cabbage, peas, and turnip followed, then steam pudding with layers of thick custard. It was all cooked in the oven of an old cast iron range with a coal-fire glowing within. The contraption was so hot it kept the whole house warm as well as giving constant hot water. It was one of the most economical forms of heating - especially as a miner got his coal for the asking.

"Didta feight int' war, Frank?" Charley said whilst we were eating.

"Aye I di' - in't Navy," I said, picking up the dialect as if I had never lost it.

"I wor a corporal in't KOYLI (Kings Own Yorkshire Light Infantry) in't first lot," said Charley, "but I were a bit old for t'second do wi' old 'Itler."

"Silly owd fool tried to volunteer an' all," said Annie.

"Aye, but they wouldn't 'ave me cos I was a collier - I was what they called Reserved - anyway they made me a Sergeant in't 'ome Guard. Me rifle was older than the one I 'ad in t'first war. It were a Ross - older than me it were!"

I left Annie and Charley a couple of hours later, and promised to write - I sent them a couple of postcards from Dartmouth. The next stop was Leeds. Where to stay? I hadn't really thought about it. I went up lower Brigate, left along Boar Lane - and there was the Griffin Hotel. I had delivered groceries there when I worked for the Co-op and always thought of it as the height of sophisticated living! It turned out to be a rather tatty pub/hotel stuck on the corner of the street. As I stopped the car a fellow in a brown weskit and peaked cap approached.

"'Ello," he said. "Are you stoppin', mister?"

"Er - well - er - yes," I said, making up my mind pronto.

"Right, lad, come on, give me yer bag," and he was away inside.

The following day I decided to try and find Cookridge Hall, never before having been there. I made my way to Adel and visited the lovely little Norman church where my forebears, the Stables, were buried, and after a few inquires made my way up to Cookridge. The Hall is a lovely old Georgian sandstone house set in well-kept grounds and now being used as a home for epileptics. Calling at the office I was met by the official in charge, and after telling him why I was interested, he very kindly took me on a tour of the place. It must have been beautiful a couple of hundred years ago. We visited the old stables too - now garages. Great-grandmother Sarah had fallen from high grace.

The *Yorkshire Post* had just finished an article on the history of the place, and my guide asked me if I would call and have a word with the editor, as he thought he would be most interested. I agreed, of course, thanking him for his kindness, and motored down the road to what was advertised as the 'Biggest Fish Shop in the World'. After a nice fishy lunch and a pint of Tetley's Ale - I went back to Leeds to meet the editor. A cup of tea was produced, he asked me about my antecedents, what I was doing now etc., took my photo, and printed it the following week. What was rather nice was the fact that I had letters later from old neighbours, schoolmates, and people who had known me thirty years before but I had long forgotten. It was a very pleasant little break and a very warming experience, quite different from the old Yorkshire rhyme:

> *Hear all and say now't*
> *Sup all and pay now't*
> *and if tha' does ow't*
> *for now't - do it for thysen.*

The Boat Show ended and I went back to Dartmouth.

A few weeks later the B.B.C. turned up again to make a further series of films for *The Onedin Line*, which had been a great success from the word go. We had a few days' filming in Hong Kong (Kingswear Station). Peter hired all the waiters he could find in the Chinese restaurants in Plymouth, Paignton & Torquay to make up the cast. There was an American Civil War episode. Another time we filmed a strike story, supposedly in Liverpool. I was one of the strike-breakers armed with a belaying pin from *The Charlotte Rhodes* - I pinched it as a souvenir of the old boat and I still have it on my mantelpiece in the mill.

It was whilst doing my bit here that I fell and hurt my back. Another day we went around to Torbay. The training ship *Denmark* was anchored off Paignton, and the script said as 'ow we had to just miss having a collision with an unknown clipper ship. With all sails set (and engine going!) we sneaked under her bow.

"Too far away!" said Peter. "Try again!"

We came about and had another go - about twenty feet away from the end of her bowsprit.

"Not close enough!" said the boss. "Have another go!"

This time I had a hand up forward who actually ducked as her jib-boom sliced through the air about six feet from our foremast stays.

"Couldn't you get a bit closer?" said the director.

"You're paying for this, guv'nor," I said. "You do it!"

He settled for what we had in the can. A couple of weeks later we went around to Exmouth, and motored through the lockgates - up the canal to Exeter, the town fathers having dredged it to ten feet for our benefit, hoping for a bit of publicity.

My back was giving me a lot of pain by then, so I was given a walk-on-and-off bit, wearing a billy-cock hat and Norfolk jacket. I used a walking stick and I had an old Irish biddy holding on to my other arm for support. I did my stint, and then I collapsed and Sylvia had to fetch me and put me to bed. The following day I was sent to Stonehouse Naval Hospital. I must have been there for about two and a half months, flat on my back with a board on top of the mattress, looking into a flexible mirror for a change of scene. One visiting day, Sylvia popped over in the Mini - gave me a kiss and a tin of Bruno tobacco, and said, "What do think? Someone has made us an offer for the business!"

"Snatch his bloody hand off!" said I.

"But we are only just starting to make any money."

"Yes, for the flipping banks - they are very happy with their twelve per cent!"

"Eleven," she said. "Anyway - you don't know what they are offering."

"Whatever it is, it's only money. You're running yourself ragged. We've been here about twelve years. It's time we had a change. Let's go to Spain."

"Spain? I love it for holidays and los toros but I've never thought of living there. What on earth would we live on?"

"Well, you could write - I could paint and do a bit of sculpture. It costs a lot less to live there than it does in England."

"You know you're not going to sail any more, don't you?"

"What do you mean?"

"I've had a word with the doctor - your sailing days are over, mate - you have to take things very carefully from now on."

"Bloody rubbish! He doesn't know what he's talking about."

But he did, and I never sailed again. And that's the nastiest phrase I've ever had to write in my life. What did we do then? We sold the business. Both boys had married now and had their own families, and our parents were no more. We went to Spain.

Chapter 34

Sylvia wanted us to live in Madrid because it is exactly the centre of Spain, and from there it is only one day's drive to anywhere. The Spanish residents say Madrid is purgatory in winter and hell in summer. Who wants to live in purgatory? We settled for Andalucia - it is only a couple of jumps to Africa, and it's always so warm. I had instructions from the doctor to swim every day, so I dutifully ambled down on my two sticks and swam, until one day Sylvia said, "Throw those bloody sticks away - you're walking like an old man!" So I did!

For some five or six years prior to leaving Dartmouth, Sylvia had been told by the doctor that unless she slowed down and took things easy she would have a real breakdown. From that time forward we had made up a programme that she organized the staffing of the Boatel and all that it entailed, and then went to Spain for four months of following the bulls in her little Mini. I was in charge, wot about that! She would go from *corrida* to *corrida* zig-zagging over Spain clocking up to twenty thousand kilometres in a season. She became so well known that she was recognised as a critic for los toros and on *Radio National de España* commented on the day's fights in English. She was the only woman ever to do this in a recognised man's world. Every year the Tourist Board invited us to any chosen *feria* in Spain - all expenses paid. I would join her in September in my Mini pickup and we would finish the taurine season together. Of course

Sylvia's Spanish by now was fluent.

Our horse we sold to a man who was crippled with polio. He was still very keen to ride but couldn't use his legs to get on a horse's back and he wanted to be quite sure it would stand perfectly still whilst he mounted. Treacle, of course, had always stood like this for Sylvia. We had planned to go and see Treacle before we left for Spain, but we received a letter from his new owner saying what a wonderful relationship had been established between them. They were "both very happy and would go together to the grave." These were his words, so - better for Tricia and ourselves - we never did go to see them.

And my lovely little *Elaine*? When I was taken off to hospital she, of course, was in Exeter. I had a friend, a Chief P.O., who very kindly sailed the boat back to Plymouth for me and put her on the mooring I rented from a local yard, telling the owner I was incapacitated, and asking him to keep her pumped out etc. The following week he was drafted abroad. Evidently, Edward Heath had turned up and my boat was shifted to accommodate his craft. *Elaine* was put on another mooring which dried out, and, of course, on the next tide she filled up - and on the next. She was hauled out and an old canvas was thrown over her and she was left like that for over three months.

One of the first things I did when I left Stonehouse was to go down to the yard and see her. Oh dear! The boat was half-full of water and the engine was covered. Sails, mattresses, and blankets were soaking wet. Most of the loose gear had been pinched. Some yob had tried to pry off the figurehead with a screwdriver. I had it fibreglassed in position but he'd made an awful mess of it. Structurally *Elaine* was sound enough, but oh, what a mess! The insurance had run out whilst I was in hospital and they didn't want to know. I threatened to sue the yard, but as there was nothing in writing, my solicitor said I hadn't a leg to stand on, which was pretty obvious - I was hopping about on two sticks. Sylvia told me that someone had offered twenty-five hundred pounds for it when I was incapacitated, but she wouldn't mention it whilst I was flat-a-back. Anyway, *Elaine* was sold for seven hundred and fifty pounds to a very nice young chap who promised to give her a good home. Oh well! Tina we left with my sister-in-law until we decided where in Spain we would settle.

We settled in Fuengirola on the Costa del Sol and rented an apartment from a lovely Spanish family. After my daily swim we would push off in the Mini up into the mountains visiting the *pueblos* that the average tourist never sees. I would do a bit of painting or sketching and Sylvia would find the Town Hall and dig out the history of the place. On our return she would type it out and clip any sketches I might have done. On impulse one day she made an appointment to see the editor of a Spanish daily newspaper, printed in English. She produced some of her work. He was delighted, and offered to take any articles she wished to sell. I started painting in earnest with the idea of holding an exhibition in one of the hotels on the coast. The editor asked if Sylvia would be willing to interview any celebrities who were on the Costa. Of course she said she would be delighted, and she had an open invitation to all the big hotels. "Come to lunch and bring your husband," or "Come over for cocktails and stay to dinner." She met titled people of all nationalities, film stars, stage celebrities, politicians etc. If I thought they may be interesting or it meant a late evening I would go along with her. We could have had a fantastic social life if we had wanted that sort of thing, but we loved the mountains and the little fishing harbours so we went socializing perhaps a couple of times a week. She interviewed Omar Sharif on many occasions. I also had the pleasure of meeting him. Names of some of the other notables we met: Bobby Moore, George Best, Sidney James, George Mitchener, Liberace, Robert Forsyth, Danny Robin, Sean Connery, Stanley Black,

Deborah Kerr etc.

Having finished a home stint of filming in Dartmouth, a couple of weeks after my return, Sylvia and I were sitting on our little patio in Fuengirola having our evening meal.

"Look, love," she said, "I've been thinking a lot about this whilst you were away. This isn't our Spain - here, is it? This isn't what we came for. The Costa del Sol is just an International Strip - people come from all over Spain to coin a fast buck. They are not the simple kindly folk we want to know. And the traffic - we might as well be in Birmingham."

"Well, what are you leading up to?"

"Do you remember that little *pueblo* I wrote about the other day? Carratraca?"

"The one with the Hermita on top of the mountain?"

"Yes, well José Maria the Practicante, told me of a disused water-mill for sale down in the valley - it could be bought very reasonably. Shall we go up and see it?"

"Yes, m'dear - why not?" Thinking - me? - in the mountains? You haven't got a prayer, mate! What about me boats? "Yes, love, we'll go tomorrow and have a picnic." Anything for a quiet life.

The following morning we made our way to Alora - the road wasn't too bad up there, but the following seventeen kilometres were awful. We met our friend in the bar, had a coffee, then climbing into the Mini, dropped down the dirt road to the Vallé de las Cañas (Valley of the Canes), parked at the old stone bridge and followed a goat path beside the stream. Big blue dragonflies were hovering as we scrambled over a waterfall, and a kingfisher flashed by us into the bushes. Striding through the high grass I tripped over a fallen tree trunk. "Hey," I said, "there's a feller in that wood," I said, looking at it with my head on one side.

"You silly old twit," said my spouse, "never mind the tree - we're here - El Molino de Los Asperones! (The Mill of the Grindstones).

It looked as though a bomb had been dropped on it. The roof had fallen in and the old iron-studded door drooped on one hinge. Hornets had made a hive in the mill-room, old wooden pulley-wheels hung off the walls, the mill-pond was dry and waist-deep in weeds and broken roof-tiles were everywhere. We walked on. There were four or five acres of land that had just been ploughed and the fruit trees appeared to be very well tended. Oranges, lemons, big black figs, plums, apricots, peaches all were in fruit. A big palm tree with golden sprays of young dates towered over us, little waterfalls were chuckling and splashing in the stream below. Behind the mill the mountain, Grajo, towered about four thousand feet and looked purple against the brilliant blue sky. A pair of golden orioles flashed over our heads, squawking at the intrusion. Two kilometres away the village hung like a splash of whitewash five hundred feet above us, its little ruined Hermita silhouetted against the sky. Further down the valley the goat-bells were tinkling.

"What do you think, love?" said my wife. "We can't afford to buy by the sea - and watching boats will be a torment."

"It's real scorpion country! Bet it's crawling with snakes," said I, tongue in cheek.

"No, really, be serious - what do you think?" she had a look in her eye like a calf gazing over a hedge at a field of clover.

"You won't have any boats but you will hear the waterfall all day long," she looked at me anxiously.

"Can't hear what you say for that bloody waterfall!" I said.

"No! Tell me! - Could you live here?"

"Well - er - reckon I could, I suppose," I said grudgingly. Her face fell.

I slipped my arm around her. "Missus, I think it's the most beautiful place I've ever seen - just wait 'til we've rebuilt it and there'll be now't like it for miles! By gum!"

It had taken us all of seven minutes to make up our minds! I can't abide people who dither about!

And what can I say about Carratraca? It is a very ordinary little *pueblo* with about one thousand inhabitants - seven hundred and fifty of whom must be kids! It is about twenty-five miles from the coast as the crow flies and about fifty miles if the crow's walking. It's not a very old *pueblo* - it was formed around 1820 around the curative springs, when the Balneario was built. The waters, however, have been used since Roman times. Lying at the junction of three older *pueblos*, Alora, Casarabonela, and Ardales, a few acres of land was subtracted from each and the village of Carratraca with its own town hall was born. The Balneario Spa came under the jurisdiction of the Counts of Teba y Montijo who had their home in the village of the latter name only twenty kilometres away. The Count had two lovely daughters, Eugenie and Francisca (Paca), and, if I may drop back with their story, you will see what influence it had on our village. William Kirkpatrick (had to be a Scot) who worked in a *bodega* in Málaga, married the daughter of a friend. Their daughter, Manuela, married and they became nobility of Spain, the Counts of Teba y Montijo. Their eldest daughter, Eugenie, who had spent her first twenty summers in the Carratraca watering-place was evidently a very lovely, vivacious person. She attracted the attention of Louis-Napoleon who was looking around for a mate of noble birth. "How can I come to you, and by which route?" asked the infatuated Louis.

"Only through the church-door," said Eugenie, blinking her violet eyes over her fluttering fan. ('Tis rumoured the title of Count was created so that Nap did not marry beneath him.) The rest is history. Her sister, Paca, married the Duke of Alba and is supposedly the model for the famous *Maja* pictures, clothed and unclothed.. With such splendid people in attendance, Carratraca became the 'in' watering-place of Spain and, indeed, of Europe. Many of the grandees built their summer homes around the Balneario, and attracted many well-known people such as Campoamor, George Sand and Lord Byron. The houses are outstandingly large for such a small *pueblo*. Surprisingly, in the 1850's Carratraca boasted three gambling casinos, twenty-odd guest houses, plus a summer palace built for King Ferdinand VII. Unfortunately, he died before residing there. It is now the Hotel El Principe. Newspapers in four languages were delivered daily by stagecoach (the *diligencia*) which ran up the Arroyo de las Cañas on the Camino Real (Royal Road). What about that then!

The story goes that, years before, Juan Mogaton (his nickname was Juan El Camison or John The Nightshirt) a bandolero, was talking to a shepherd. Juan had a dreadful disease, he was covered in sores and could only wear this loose flowing garment.

"Why don't you bathe in the waters of Carratraca?" said the sheepman. "Always I dip my animals in the pools and they are the healthiest sheep in the valley. It doesn't cost anything - why not try it?"

Juan took his advice, bathed in the curative waters and was healed. Delighted and very thankful, he built a small shrine halfway up the mountain to Nuestra Señora de Salud, the Patrona of Health-giving Waters, and being a good Spanish bandit prayed to her regularly when he placed his pot of flowers in the little sanctuary.

Doña Trinidad Grund was the daughter of the German iron-maker who built the first blast-furnaces in Málaga, and she married into the Heredia family who owned most of the town. Widowed and coming back from Germany from a family visit the sailing-ship was wrecked near Gibraltar. She was pulled ashore only to find that she had lost all her three children. Naturally she was in a dreadful state and the doctors suggested that she go to Carratraca to the house of her in-laws to take the waters and recuperate. This she did, recovered, and, loving the place, built a home. Trinidad Grund became a benefactress to the village, indeed to all Málaga. She built the old bullring which was carved into the mountains (it could have been a Roman theatre).

The subterranean stalactite cave, La Gruta, she renovated, had steps carved in the rock, and fitted it with gas lighting. There are neolithic paintings in the grotto, discovered by Abbe Breuille. The benefactress designed and built a lovely little Hermita on top of the mountain. Unfortunately on the day of its inauguration it was struck by a thunderbolt and practically destroyed. The four walls still stand and can be seen for miles around.

Trinidad Grund's house, in Franco's time, became a boarding-school, for girls brought in from the countryside for eight months of the year for eight or nine years of basic education. The house in recent years has become a rather splendid Ayuntamiento - town hall.

With only the stony river-crossing, Camino Real, leading to it, once Empress Eugenie and the grandees left - the Carratraca watering-place sank into obscurity, as did many other spas at the time. A new road was made to Alora and the Spa opened again as now, for the summer months, for the suffering to cure their rheumatism. The cures are many. Now - a splendid roadway leads to and from Málaga to Carratraca and its popularity was regained to a degree.

It was decided - we would buy the Molino de las Asperones. We started the usual, long process of bargaining aided by José Maria, the Practicante. Spain, especially if one is an *extranjero*, one never dickers with the owner - a third person should always be used. The proprietor knows how much he wants. You know how much you are prepared to pay. If he wants fifteen, he asks twenty. You will pay fifteen but start at ten. This is all fun for them, when you remember the Arabs were here for nearly eight hundred years and they left their mark in many ways. It took three months to arrange but eventually we got it for fifteen - he was quite happy - just the price he'd reckoned on! The Alcalde's son was a newly qualified surveyor. He drew up the house-plans to make it official. The Ayuntamiento put a rubber stamp on them. After that no one ever looked at them again. We wanted to keep as much of the original building as possible but the builders were dead against it. "Look, Frank," the boss said, "it's only built of mud and stone and as long as it's *cal*'d every year it will be okay. But in the state it's in now it would be asking for trouble. To *cal* is to limewash and every house in Andalucia is painted with this at least once a year - not for aesthetic reasons, as I had always thought, but because it's very necessary. This work is always done by women - no man worth his salt would touch a *cal*-brush! So we took the mill down, stone by stone and rebuilt it on the same curtilage with reinforced concrete foundations, making the original doorways and windows and using the same stone, but, of course, cementing it. The pond and the *riego* had to be cleaned out first to give us water to make the concrete. The *riego* is a small canal which taps the main stream about a kilometre away, follows the contour of the hillside and gives water to four other *fincas* for irrigation purposes. Before we could start building we had to get Paco the tractor to cut a road where the goat track used to be, through the trees and bushes up to the house.

We used local labour, of course, and all work was done by hand. A single whip was used to lift the buckets of cement which, again, was mixed manually. I suggested that we hire a small hoist and cement-mixer but the idea was turned down flat, and the *peónes* carried all these great stones by hand up the rickety ladder. The weather was scorching hot and their gloved hands were no doubt blistering as they toiled up and down, but no one grumbled and, as we brought a crate of beer with us each time we came, they were quite happy. The old window-frames and doors were rotten, of course, and the roof tiles and the *lozas de barro* - many of the original clay floor-tiles were broken, so we visited Peñarrubia, a deserted village in the National Park scheduled to be inundated when the new dam was finished.

One of our great delights always is the National Park, about seven kilometres away from Carratraca. Situated in fantastic mountain scenery and surrounded by pine forests, the three great man-made lakes shine deep emerald in the sunshine. I assume that it is the clay soil that makes them so green, and, strangely enough, there are no weeds in the lakes, although they are well stocked with fish. This is where we bathe, and it's like swimming in milk. Camping is free and barbecues, toilets, drinking water, firewood, rustic tables and seats are all provided.

Peñarrubia had been abandoned and the people settled in other villages as the water gradually rose to fill the last of the *pantanos*. Antonio Campano, a bright young man from Ardales, had bought the whole ruined *pueblo*. He was in the process of demolishing it and selling the materials when we arrived. "Oh, you are the *extranjeros* from Carratraca, si? You are rebuilding the molino in the Valley de las Cañas, si?" As we were the only foreigners in the village our fame had gone before us. We smiled and asked permission to look around. He waved his hand - "Take anything you need - just put a chalk mark on it and I'll get a man to move it into the church. It won't cost you much - we are delighted to see you. I shall have to charge for the transport as well, though." We wandered around the village. It was pathetic. Lovely old cottages were being pushed down by bulldozer. Old iron studded doors, tables, chairs, plates and old chests were buried under the rubble. Everything there had been made by hand. The same families had lived there for hundreds of years. I dragged out half a dozen *piletas*, animal food troughs laboriously chiselled by hand out of blocks of local marble. Some of the others were six feet square - they must have taken weeks of work - but we would have needed a crane to lift them. We rescued two big iron-studded doors made of two-inch pine, three pairs of *celosias* - cupboard doors with the traditional hatched ventilators, folding window-frames with shutters, a pair of big handmade cattle branding-irons - out of which I later made candlesticks, a lovely little round-topped 'dot' chest into which some girl had once carefully folded her handmade sheets. A broken doll lay in the gutter. Wisps of tinsel hung in a corner - a fragment of last Christmas. We were both choked by the enormity of it. There was a poor old chap sitting on a broken rust-bottomed chair, his chin resting on his walking stick, his old dog by his side. "I was born here seventy odd years ago, my family has lived here for generations," he said sadly. "I shall stay here until the water comes over my feet - if I don't die first." I made some sketches of the village and the old man with the dog, intending to use them in an oil painting to be called, 'Death of a Pueblo'. I still have them but can't bring myself to use them. We picked up dozens of thick red floor tiles, cement stuck on the bottom and shining on top with years of polishing. The heavy iron bars - *rejas* - which all the houses have over their windows in Spain were no doubt made by the local blacksmith. We bought these by the kilo weight, and dozens of heavy Roman roof tiles. We sorted out five or six *cántaros* - enormous Ali Baba earthenware oil jars for Sylvia to use for flowerpots. Between us we pulled out a door frame. There were two doors in it, each having eight small panes of handmade glass with pine shutters behind. There must have been forty coats of paint on it. Later I burned it off and scraped them. They are lovely. We chalked a cross on everything we needed - we felt like grave-robbers. Thanking Antonio, we climbed back into the car. Neither of us said very much on the way back home. We drove past the village a few years later. All that was left was the ruin of the little church with its rusty iron cross on top of the steeple, and a sad old palm tree sticking out of the water. Peñarrubia - The Red Cliff.

We were still living in Fuengirola whilst the *molino* was being built but we came up each weekend to watch progress, staying at Pepa's *fonda* overnight. The old pine doors etc. were lashed on top of our Mini and we took them back with us to Fuengirola, burned off forty coats of paint, sanded and varnished them and stowed them away until needed. Pepa's *fonda* is known all over the province. She is a very big lady and the best cook for miles around. Her meals are all traditionally Andalusian - there are always three huge courses with as many helpings as one could wish for and as much wine as one can drink and the cost is one third of what one would pay on the Costa. Nothing 'fazes' her. Anything from seventy to one hundred people turn up at weekends - no one ever books - and Pepa herself does all the cooking on a big gas stove with two or three village girls doing the chores. (I always eat too much!)

The *bandera*, the Spanish flag, was hoisted and fixed when the chimney was fitted on the mill at the end of June and the roof finished. Pepa provided a traditional and huge meal for all the workers which I brought down in the car with crates of beer, wine and a couple of bottles of 'wicky'. Not being a drinking crowd, the workers were soon all singing like birds. A couple of weeks later we ran out of money. The Harold Wilson government had put the damper on things and British nationals were only allowed to bring fifty pounds at one time out of the country. Four thousand pounds was eventually permitted to those intending to 'settle' and any other monies were frozen for four years. Three cheers for King Harold! We managed to fiddle another thousand pounds by swapping a cheque with a friend going back to the U.K. - after that we were skint. We told the builders to leave the ground floor unfinished and stop work at the end of the week. "But we haven't finished yet," said Antonio.

We said they would have to work for now't if they didn't - so they stopped.

Most of the main work was done, however, except for fitting doors, windows, painting, which we could do, and the general cleaning of the site which, of course, now looked again like the quarry we saw originally. Our furniture, mostly second-hand, six boxes of books and other odds and sods were stacked on the bare earth of the ground floor as we couldn't yet afford to have it tiled. All the woodwork was as it came from the carpenters, the plumbers had finished, *Gracias a Dios*, so we had water, a gas stove, a bathroom, a small gas refrigerator and gas lamps for light. We had been promised electricity by Christmas. Ha! We then moved in and started really the happiest years of our lives.

Three pairs of nightingales we have to sing us to sleep, and when the sun comes up each morning it touches Trinidad's Hermita and turns it to gold. The rest of the valley is in shadow, but as the sun rises the village above us turns from gold - to pink - to white. Grajo, our mountain, changes colour all day long, from gold to yellow to ochre, its shadows from black to purple to violet, then from blue to lavender. Grajo is so high that a man cannot see all the way to the top - it takes a man and a boy. The waterfall chuckles away below us. We have twenty-two different kinds of fruit. Our water is free - it comes out of the side of the mountain, clean, sweet and icy cold. We now have twelve-volt solar lighting so we pay no electric bills. The 'telly' is also twelve-volt and in Spain there is no licence to pay. We have all the firewood we want - we grow it. We have hundreds of trees and I have a name for every one of them. I love my trees! At the time of writing our rates and taxes cost fifty-three pounds per annum. Never a week passes without one of us saying to the other "Aren't we lucky!"

Chapter 35

It was about this time that we met Michael Limb. He became Publicity Manager of the Patronato de Turismo, and thus worked for twenty years or more with Sylvia, writing to increase tourism. At our introduction, I said "Michael Limb." (note the surname) "Did you come from Dewsbury Road, Leeds?"

He looked astonished, and said, "Yes, my grandfather was an undertaker there."

"Your grandfather buried my father," I almost stammered with surprise. "And he didn't send Mother a bill for it, as she was skint."

From 1972 on, Michael, his wife, June, and children Helen, Jason, and Cassandra became visitors to El Molino as 'family', and, not long after, they became neighbours. Michael bought 5,000 ms. of our land - stuck a lovely caravan (an old British Coal Board display van) near trees by the stream. Most weekends brought them to Carratraca.

Sylvia thumped away on the typewriter daily, turning out thirty or so articles a month. I hadn't yet properly fitted the glass double-doors we had bought from Peñarrubia and the swallows flew in and out of the lounge all day long, much to our delight. We were presented with a couple of kittens which pleased Tina no end and she lay and suckled them for hours - that she didn't have any milk didn't seem to matter anyway - she didn't look for any difference between puppies and kittens. She loved baby-sitting!

I fitted shelves, doors and windows, shifted rocks, planted geraniums, made a lawn, and, with all the bricks and stones we had left over, made a workshop. I fitted a bench, and a vice I bought from the local scrapyard for three hundred pesetas. We lived on what Sylvia earned and what few pieces of work I managed to turn out.

The tree trunk that I tripped over on our first visit to the *finca*, I hauled into my workshop and from it carved a life-sized figure of St. Francis of Assisi with birds sitting on his outstretched hand. This I presented to Sylvia for her birthday and he stood on a great rock in front of the house. One evening we were sitting on the patio having a drink when my wife said, "Northy, all these years - not only have you been fooling me, but you've been fooling yourself."

"What do you mean?"

"It wasn't sailing you were in love with was it? It was boats!"

"Wait a minute!"

"No! You wait! Why did you love a boat? Because it's made of wood - and you could cut it and carve it and create it! A new shiny glass-fibred yacht with aluminium masts and lots of stainless steel is much more efficient! And there is much less labour attached to it - and you wouldn't give tuppence for it, would you?"

Silence.

"You have been scouring and planning, building, cementing, making rookeries, carving St. Francis - and never once have you missed your sailing, have you? Be honest!"

Silence.

"Are you happy here? Is there anything you want more? - Do you want money? Do you want anything?"

"Apart from some three-inch screws and a new half-inch chisel, no." I grinned. "Do you want ow't?"

"Only that typing table you keep going to make out of the baby chair you picked up at the dump. Can't think of anything else."

And together we both said, "Aren't we lucky!"

It was on a Saturday afternoon, it was raining, we were on our way to Carratraca when Minnie hit a pothole full of water. It was deeper than we thought. Sylvia was driving and she over-corrected. We bounced and shot across the verge thirty yards down the forty-five degree slope the other side. Fortunately for us there were a lot of stiff broom bushes growing in our path and we slowly stopped - two feet away from a very large boulder!

"Pssss!"

"Have you got your hand-brake on?"

"Yes," she whispered.

"Cut the engine."

It died.

"Put her in reverse."

"It's in."

We were talking out of the sides of our mouths as any loud noise might shake Minnie.

"Open your door carefully and don't shake the car!"

We crept out, then climbed up to the top of the bank. When we had driven over the top there wasn't a soul in sight, but when we got to the rim of the hump we found three thousand Spaniards jumping up and down and waving their arms, and all shouting advice. A middle-aged gentleman took me by the arm.

"You won't get a *grua* (crane) today - you'll need a tractor for that," he said, pointing to Minnie who was standing nearly on her nose.

"I reckon," I said, scratching my head.

"Hop in my *coche*," he said pointing to his car.

We climbed in and he roared off down the road. Three kilometres later he turned into a farmyard. Jumping out he walked up to the door of the house.

"Hola," he said, opened the door and walked in.

The old farmer was having his 'dins' at the table and watching football on the telly. He looked rather startled.

"There's an *extranjero* here," my companion said, "his *coche* has gone over the bank and he needs a tractor - have you got one?"

"Si," said t'owd feller, "it's down the lane - but I'm having my lunch."

"Never mind that," said my companion. "It's raining and his wife is getting wet. Come on!"

The old chap looked a bit blank, his shoulders touched his ears and he pushed away his plate. Up he got, shouted something incomprehensible to his son, picked up an umbrella, walked back with us, and climbed into the car. We drove back to the waiting crowd of Spaniards. Then, minutes later, came the tractor driven by his son. The farmer fumbled around the back of the vehicle, struggling with his umbrella and handed me a tatty splintery old wire rope. I slithered down the bank, wrapped it around the Mini, packed it with our towels and swimsuits and ow't else I could find, tied a big bowline on it and tossed the other end up to the farmer who shackled it on to the machine. It took the strain, and slowly the car backed up the steep slope. As the wheels came into sight all the crowed shouted "Olé!" Everybody shook hands with everybody else, the farmer was congratulated, Sylvia and I were thumped on the back and wished *mucha suerte* and they all drove off talking excitedly. My good Samaritan with the car waved away my thanks, wished me well and drove away. Coiling up the wire I walked to the farmer, "Mil gracias, señor," I said, "cuanto me debo?"

He frowned, wagged his finger under my nose and said, "Na!" Pointing to his chest he said, "Ese es mi satisfacción!"

"Señor," I said, "please let me pay you for your trouble."

"Hombre," said the old man, "if this happened in your country any *campesino* would have done the same, na?"

I wonder. (I did manage to slip his son a mil pesetas when he wasn't looking.)

Coming back from Alora one day a few weeks later the old car started sparking. "Sod it," I said, climbing out and lifting the bonnet. At that moment another car passed me, stopped and backed up.

"Que pasa?" said the driver.

"Oh, it's not much, just a dirty plug - but I haven't got a plug spanner with me."

"Momento, señor!" he fumbled around in his car boot, picked up a roll of spanners and threw them to me. "You'll find one to fit there," he said. "Sorry I can't stop to help, I'm in rather a hurry - leave the tools at the next bar on the left and I'll pick them up later. Mucha suerte!" - And he was away.

I'd never seen the chap before in my life and, as far as I knew, he didn't know me from Adam! Viva España! (He was the local doctor, we found out later.)

That autumn Tina joined us; Sylvia's sister brought her over from England. Brother-in-law Bill had made a big Doggie box which he dragged from the plane, past the noses of the customs officers without even stopping - much to their amazement, out into the reception lounge.

We did see a couple of very long snakes whilst we were building - not that they took any notice of us, but never having had much to do with the creatures - well, I wondered. As it happened, a young South African had just opened a Snake Pit in Torremolinas and, nothing loath (whatever that may mean), Sylvia decided that she would do an article on it. The owner was delighted with the idea of a free bit of publicity and perhaps Sylvia would like a photo of himself with the cobra?

"Of course," said her ladyship and took out the camera whilst the owner picked up the snake and put it down at her feet. Sylvia was adjusting the lens when the cobra flattened its head - made a beeline for her, then ducked into a nearby flower-bed. Using a couple of forked sticks the owner picked it up and put it back into its cage, whereupon it promptly spat a stream of venom over the glass front. "Oh," said Sylvia, "I thought you always 'milked' them!"

"Oh, no," said the keeper, "but he is a bit bad-tempered - let's try the boa constrictor." He pulled it out of its cage and it promptly curled around him pinioning his arms and legs. She got two or three good pictures. He grinned apologetically, "Sorry to ask you but I'm afraid you'll have to help me - just unwind him, will you?"

Looking a bit startled, she grabbed its tail and walked around until the owner could grab its head and pop it back into the box. I would have helped, but he didn't ask me!

"What is this big one called, then," said Sylvia, "a python?" It was curled up in its cage fast asleep (that's the way I like them) and it had four hamsters tucked away in its coils. "I thought he are these things," she said. "Aren't they frightened?"

"No, he won't touch them unless he's hungry. He's sloughing his skin - he's got a couple of weeks yet."

"We are living in the *campo*," I said (over the wall) - "We've seen a couple of snakes about four feet long, would it be wise to always wear boots?"

He laughed. "No, not in Spain. Forget 'em! There are some snakes about but they are all perfectly harmless. All a snake wants is a quiet life - when they hear you coming they will push off. There is a small black viper who lives on the mountain-tops, he is poisonous, if you tread on him he'll attack in self-defence, but when he feels the vibrations of your feet he'll go away immediately. Snakes - forget 'em!"

Mind you, mention reptiles to any Spaniard and he will tell you that his aunt, grandma, cousin or some female member of his family was feeding a child at her breast when she went to sleep, and lo! when she woke - there was a snake suckling at her bosom! The times I've heard that story! (It happens in every family - must do!)

Chapter 36

It was early in July and very hot, so we decided to go camping along the Atlantic coast of Portugal. Sylvia was talking on the phone to one of her friends, the editor of *Guidepost*, a magazine printed in English and published weekly in Madrid. Douglas Boyd is a Scot with a French/Spanish wife and three lovely children.

"Lucky old you," said Doug when she told him of our plans. "It's sizzling up here in the Big City. Poor old Nieves is going barmy trying to keep the kids cool - they're on holiday, of course, for the next couple of months."

"Douglas," said Sylvia, "why don't you bring them all down here and take over the *finca* whilst we are away? You can look after my cats and feed the old cocker spaniel, Tina. She'll be happier at home than flopping about in the back of the Mini."

"Sylvia," said Doug, "what a grand idea - I'll have a word with Nieves and phone you back! Right!"

It was all arranged, and a couple of days later we were packing the camping gear on Minnie when their motor horn sounded down the lane. This was a period 'between bridge', and the water in the stream luckily was reduced to a trickle as it was being used for irrigation higher up the valley. I went across, up the far bank to help with the kids and handing up the baggage to Doug, on the home side. I peeped into the car to see if anything had been left behind, then I looked again. "Oye, Douglas!" I shouted. "You've got a corpse in the back of your car!"

"Is the old chap dead then?"

"Well, he looks like it."

"Wait a minute." He came back over the stream and peered inside. "No, I don't think he's dead, he always looks like that." He opened the door and prodded the cadaver-like figure. It opened one eye and then shut it again. He turned to me and said, "No, he's still with us. Sorry, mate, I forgot to tell you, Nieves has brought her father along, he is turned eighty and lives with us. We couldn't leave the old chap behind and I expect he has taken an extra Valium pill - he's always doing that. You don't mind?"

"No, of course not, poor old feller, but we have to get him over the stream and up the other bank. It's about another hundred yards to the house."

We wrestled the old man out of the car and lifted him between us across the stream and over the slope on the other side.

"You don't have a stretcher, of course," said Douglas, wiping his forehead.

"No," I said, "but wait a minute!"

Going up to the house I came back trundling my wheelbarrow with a mattress on it. We picked up Grandad and laid him down with a leg on each side of the barrow.

"Who's going to push him up the slope?" said Douglas.

"You are, mate - it's yer old feller - you're the best bugger to push him."

We got him up to the house and laid him down in the cool of the mill, whereupon he opened his eyes and said in very unaccented English, "I am so sorry to have caused you all this inconvenience." Sylvia was down with us by then and clucked over him like a mother hen. Anyway, after showing them around the house and explaining how the pump worked, we left them and pushed off to Portugal.

We had a really fine holiday and made our way back,

crossing the border into Spain again, in the direction of Badajoz when unfortunately a passing lorry flicked up a stone and smashed the windscreen. Sod it! Knocking out the broken pieces of glass we hurried down to the provincial capital. It was six forty-five in the evening when we at last found a garage. Crossing my fingers I went into the office.

"Buenas, señor," I said hopefully, "do you have a windscreen for a Mini?"

"A Mini Toro?" said the garage owner.

"Si." (It had the old Morris Contey badge on the radiator with a cow on it and in Spain it was always known as a Mini Toro.)

"That's the one with the Málaga number plate? Si?"

"Si."

"And I suppose you want it fixed right away so that you can get back to the Costa del Sol? No?"

"Si," I said. "Have you got one then?"

"Yes, I have got one as it happens, but it's seven o'clock on a Saturday night."

Looking suitably pathetic, I started to explain how important it was that I get back etc. He let me burble on for a while and then he grinned.

"I'll feex it for you, señor."

"Mooochas gracias!" I beamed. "Er - um, er - how long do you think it will take er - um?"

"Just as long as it take you to have a coffee - about twenty minutes."

Would you believe? Saturday night and all! In half an hour we were on our way south with a new windscreen, which, with the labour and a tip cost us six thousand pesetas!

It was obvious we shouldn't make it back to Carratraca that night so we stopped at Jabugo in Huelva, a village famous for its home-cured hams. Eighteen years previously we had stayed at the hostel for one night on our way back to England. We rang the bell.

"Do you remember they had a young vine on the patio and we helped ourselves to grapes for breakfast?" said Sylvia.

Pit a pat, pit a pat, footsteps on the stairs. The door opened. The Señora stopped, looked at us, then beamed!

"Mis Ingleses! Si? Dios mio!" She put her arms around us and kissed us on both cheeks. Turning and talking at the same time, she literally pulled us up the stairs. "You sent me cards for Navidad - oo! Muchas años pasado, si? I've still got them!" she cried.

Half an hour later we were still talking over tapas and a jar of wine, sitting under the grapevine now as thick as my leg. The following morning she proudly escorted us around the village, re-introducing us to her little boy - now about six foot two with a family of his own, and a big cool underground store holding thousands of hams (patas negras) black feet - the best! More wine and tapas, then we left her waving to us as we sped down the road to Seville. We stopped to telephone Anna Marie at the village store and inquire about Douglas and his family.

"Pues," said Anna Marie. "Bien. We had the funeral yesterday and I think the family are going back to Madrid tomorrow."

"Funeral?" squealed Sylvia. "Whose funeral?"

"El Viejo - the Old One - naturalmente!" said Anna Marie.

We pressed on as fast as we could home, where Nieves poured out the whole story.

Douglas had gone back to Madrid (working, he came down at weekends) and she was alone with the children when her father died, very quietly in his sleep. She sent the two boys up to the *pueblo* for the doctor, whereupon they were immediately scooped up and taken care of by the villagers. The *alcalde* came down to the house to watch over the body whilst the men organised the coffin, transport, etc. Then it was taken away and put into the 'Tele Club' - the only public T.V. room in the village, where the women sat with Nieves, plying her with brandy until she fell asleep, whereupon she was carried to the house next door and put to bed. After a short service the following day the old man was buried in the cemetery, and Douglas came down that evening and took the family back to Madrid. Nieves had previously told Sylvia that her French father was a baron, and although not a Nazi, had served with the Vichy Government. At the end of the war he came to the Pyrenees with a Jewish woman and settled in Spain where she, illegitimate, Nieves, was born. He was supposedly a very wealthy man and had entertained lavishly. End of story.

However, some months later, out of the blue, we were sent a cutting from *Herald Tribune*.

FRENCH COLLABORATOR
DIES UNNOTICED

Carratraca, Málaga, Spain.

Self-styled Baron Louis Darquier de Pellepoix, the French Commissioner for Jewish Affairs in Nazi-Occupied France recently died unnoticed in this small village near Málaga. Between 1942 and 1944 he deported 75,000 Jews to death-camps. He was dismissed by the Government of Occupied France for embezzling Jewish property. At the end of the war he fled to Spain, always maintaining that the Nazis never exterminated Jews. A French court sentenced him to death *in absentia* in 1947 for espionage for a foreign power.

In 1978 a French journalist interviewed him for *L'Express* and he talked about Auschwitz, the Nazi death-camp. 'They used gas, yes, but only for the lice when they disinfected the prisoner's garments. The statement that six million Jews were exterminated was pure fabrication! Jewish lies! As for photographs of emaciated bodies stacked up in the camps or being pushed by bulldozers into burial pits - the photos were faked! Jews are like that!'

In 1937 he became President of the Anti-Jewish Committee of France and worked with German anti-Semites on his programme 'The Jews must be expelled or massacred'. His affectations included an aristocratic *de* to his name, always wearing riding boots and breeches, and sporting a monocle. He was named Commissioner-General of Jewish Affairs in May 1942, but was dismissed in February 1944 for embezzling funds left behind by deported Jews.*

The above announcement came only weeks after the jailing of Klaus Barbie, a Gestapo Chief, after his expulsion from Bolivia.

'Baron' Darquier 'de' Pellepoix - the polite old gentleman we had trundled up the drive in a wheelbarrow! How fall the mighty!

"My father must have been a congenital liar," she told Sylvia. "I am knee-deep in reporters. Write what you like, use photos - I don't care any more," and got off the phone.

"I shall not write anything," said my love, "I am so sad for them all - especially the children. Their Grandpa!"

---

* All monies were confiscated and Nieves was left poor.

Chapter 37

Southern Spain is always short of water. We never have enough. Usually there are two or three years of semi-drought, then fortunately the Heavens open up and we'll have *tormentas* for a week or ten days. It really pours! Fifty to seventy litres per square metre in twenty-four hours. Double in some parts of Spain. That's a lot of rain. We, however, are very lucky having our own spring for drinking water and the stream for irrigation. They both come out cold and clear straight from the mountainside. We'd lived in the Molino for about three years before the tormentas hit us. The sound of three metres of water roaring down our valley was a bit 'skeery' at first, but as the house sits about sixty feet up the hillside, it was obvious we should be quite safe. Tree trunks and fence posts come swivelling past with the roaring sound of boulders tumbling along beneath the flood.

Forty-eight hours later the sun was shining and the stream was down to normal, but the little ford we used to cross at the entrance to the *finca* with a gap of about ten feet had gone, leaving a five foot deep hole between two huge boulders. The car, of course, was on the wrong side of the river. Silly old Mini. However with Sylvia helping, I cut down ten poplar trees and laid them across the hole. Then we put the bigger branches 'thwartships and nailed them on to the tree trunks. T'owd car went across beautifully, and with the odd repair the bridge lasted for two or three years until the next floods when it went sailing down to Málaga and the deep blue sea.

So we parked the car in the lane again and used a couple of stepping stones to cross the stream.

There is a huge rock at the entrance to the *finca* with a cave inside it. I sculpted a little Virgin about three feet high and she lives in the cave, and if we fail to do so, the village children put flowers into a little vase which she holds in her hands. I'm not a particularly religious person but it's just a little offering to the Good Lord for the trees and flowers and birds and all the happiness that we have found here.

One day I was giving her some fresh flowers when a little voice behind me said, "Hola, buenos días." I turned and saw a little boy about nine years old.

"Hola, chico," I said. "Como estas? Bien?"

"Sí, señor, gracias." A pause, then he looked sideways at me. "You are not a Spanish man, are you?" he queried.

"No, I come from Inglaterra."

"Oh," pause. "Do you get any letters from there?"

Oh! Oh! "Why, chico, do you save stamps?"

He looked rather shy, then grinned. "Sí."

"Well., we'll go and have a look - I may have one or two."

Sylvia has a 'thingy' about stamps, for guide-dogs - tears them off every letter we get and has fat envelopes full of them. The little boy went away looking very happy, with a fist full of stamps and a tum full of Coca-Cola.

Later that summer Sylvia was commissioned to write an article for D.F.D. Seaways, a Danish ferry service which plied between Málaga and Genoa. We loaded Minnie with all our gear and camping equipment and trundled on board the *Dana Corona* where she lay in the port of Málaga. We were given fine accommodation and Sylvia was delighted with the fruit and flowers sent to our cabin by the Captain. Cruising along at eighteen knots there was a short stay in Ibiza then away again to dine in Genoa, where as soon as we docked, we headed south for Rome. What can I say about Rome that hasn't already been said? We loved it! Neither of us had been there before. The *autostradas* of course were marvellous after using our Spanish country roads. But the Italian drivers! My Gawd! They were worse than the Andaluz. Anyway, it was a wonderful holiday with all expenses paid - one of the perks of being married to a journalist!

Working on the *finca* a few weeks later a young man crossed the stream on the stepping stones.

"Buenos días, señor," he said. "I'm cutting down the poplar trees further down the valley. Do you want to sell any of your trees? I'll give you a good price."

There was a pair of golden orioles nesting in one of mine and anyway, I don't like cutting down trees - they take too long to grow, besides which, I know all my trees by name.

"No, señor, I don't want to sell any timber - But - " I stopped and pondered. "Could you cut down those two eucalyptus?" pointing to them. They were about sixty feet high and about three feet thick - lovely trees and I hated the thought of doing it. "I want them for a bridge across here," and I showed him where my original bridge had been. "However, you will have to drop them at an angle, I don't want them falling on my little Virgin."

He looked at the trees and then to where I wanted them placed. "Sí," he said. "No hay problemas, I'll get my saw and do it now." The big motor saw screamed as it bit into the wood. My lovely trees shuddered, groaned with anguish, and one by one the beauties fell with a mighty crash across the stream. He trimmed the branches, carefully cutting out two or three crooks I wanted for carving, then 'topped' them.

"Perfecto," said I. "There's enough firewood here to see me through the winter. Now then, how much do I owe you?"

He smiled, "You are Ingles? Sí?"

"Sí."

"Then you are the *caballero* who gave my son a lot of stamps for his collection. Sí?"

"Sí," I said, remembering the little boy.

"Well, I should think that only pays for your kindness, señor. It gives me pleasure to help you - siempre - any time!"

We shook hands and he left me with my fallen giants. The remainder of the timber I cut into portable lengths with my little power saw and piled it on the river bank. That left the two huge tree trunks to be moved into position. The bottom of the stream was littered with big rocks, so shifting the trees wasn't going to be easy. That evening I hailed Miguel as he was going home from the next *finca*.

"Hola, chico, will you and your amigos give me a hand to shift these" - pointing to the trees.

He looked at them. "Hombre - No! We are not insured for that sort of thing - muy peligroso (too dangerous)!"

I looked at him in amazement, opened my mouth, then shut it again. "Sod you, mate!" I said in English. As my old mentor Hornblower would have said, 'One British tar is equal to five Frogs or ten pesky Dons.' "Right!" I said airily - "Forget it, I'll do it myself!"

His jaw dropped and he looked at me in amazement - they must have weighed about five tons each.

"Well, not entirely on my own. Sylvia will give me a hand. Pues! Hasta Manaña!"

I walked away towards the house. Why don't you keep your big mouth shut, Northy, I thought. You're stuck with it now. This is one time you can't lose face. If I said tomorrow and I couldn't do it, Miguel would be delighted. He would do it - even if it killed him. Previously I had asked his father, Raphael, to help me lift a big rock that had fallen across the path.

"Na!" he said, "I'll do it!" He's a skinny little man - nothing of him at all.

"You'll give yourself a rupture, you silly old twit," I said. As I bent down he pushed me to one side.

"Na! Yo!" He got his arms around it and staggered a few

steps across the path, his old knees knocking together, then he dropped it over the bank. Then he swaggered off again. Spanish pride! (He had a double hernia a few weeks later.)

I had scrounged some heavy lift wires from a hotel on the coast - soaked in grease and very strong and very flexible. These I used as parbuckles with a heavy pair of blocks tailed onto them, a big handy-bill. was then clamped onto the lot. Making a ramp out of heavy branches with both Sylvia and me hauling, the downstream trunk gradually climbed up over the other one. Where they came into contact with the other tree I packed it with slippery green watercress, then with a final heave it skidded over and rolled five yards upriver in the right direction. That was the principle I worked on. It took a time but I was in no hurry. With a lever here and a push there, they gradually climbed over each other upstream until I got them into position. The butts then had to be lifted up five feet onto the bank. No hoist. Job stopped! Ten days later about ten young students from Málaga University came camping in the valley. One of them asked if he could buy some of my cherries. Sharp as a razor I am!

"Bring some buckets and take all the cherries you want," says I. "But get your friends to give me a hand to lift these tree-trunks for ten minutes first, okay?"

"Vale!" said the young man. "Y muchas gracias!"

So that's how we did it. I hate picking cherries anyway!

Sylvia then went down to Alora railway station, chatted up the foreman, and bought forty old sleepers for fifty pesetas each. The local blacksmith made us eighty iron spikes. I was rather dreading having to bore holes for them with my old hand-brace, but fortunately the original plate holes came in just the right place. The spikes were bashed in with a seven pound hammer, and the job was done! Olé! Just to make sure that it doesn't float off to Málaga like the other one, I lashed both ends of the bridge to the neighbouring rocks with the lift wires then seized the ends back. Now every time we get a bucketful of rain I'm asked if my bridge is still there. Miguel and his mates would love it to float away! Someone must have told him about old Horny (Horatio Hornblower).

Chapter 38

Christmas Day in Spain is definitely a family affair, and apart from the presents to the children things in the *pueblo* are very quiet. The festivities go on right through to Noche Vieja (the Night of the Old Year) when the whole country makes whoopee. The big day for the children however is January 5th when the Three Kings (Night of the Three Kings) come to every town and village in the country. In the big towns there is a magnificent carnival parade where the Kings - clad in gorgeous robes, carry presents for the youngsters, borne on beautiful floats and, with their helpers, throw sweets and toys to the kids. There are great processions with lots of brass bands, decorated elephants, camels, clowns and ponies. Each parish in the town tries to outdo the others. No expense is ever spared! Businessmen give vast sums of money to charity to have the privilege of being one of the Kings on that great day. Santa Claus and Christmas trees were unknown before the *extranjeros* brought the idea with them to Spain - now there is a Father Christmas and a decorated tree even in the smallest *pueblo*. Our first Christmas in the Molino was a delight. We decorated the house with pine branches from Grajo, (the mountain above us), and we had a roaring log fire, the timber from our own trees.

The weather was beautiful with the sun shining down from a clear blue sky, but there was a cold wind blowing from the Sierra Nevada. (Sierra meaning 'saw-toothed' and Nevada is the name for snow - looking at the peaks in the distance one can see how the name came to be.) In the afternoon we collected bunches of white jonquils - a paper-white narcissus which grows wild on the hillside across the valley. The following day Pedro the Alcalde and Miguelin, his town clerk, came down to wish us the compliments of the season. Sylvia was given a bottle of liqueur and I was given a bottle of Fundador cognac and a large parcel. Opening this, I found it contained a film-extra cowboy outfit - sombrero, six shooters and a sheriff's star, as well as a paper from the Ayuntamiento, signed by the Alcalde and all the elders of the village appointing me officially 'Sheriff de la Paz' of the 'Arroyo de las Cañas'. What about that! I'm very proud of that piece of paper and it's framed and hung where all can see it.

Having no electricity nearer than the village when we first moved into the Molino, we used bottled gas for cooking, lighting and fridging. There was a great to-do when the 110 volts in Carratraca was changed to 220. One morning some days later (it was raining) I had occasion to go up and collect some mail. I parked the car and strolled into the plaza. Our one village copper was standing with his thumbs in his gunbelt - beaming! - he had been here for twenty-seven years and never had an arrest.

"Que pasa, Salvador - how goes it?" I enquired.

"Muy bueno, Frank - fantástico! Look!" he said pointing. "Now we have power in the *pueblo*!"

Bloody great sparks were flashing down the walls - across the street and up the other side! The old 110 volt wires were still drooping in clusters from the walls of the houses, never having been renewed and the kids were having a high old time dodging the sparks!

"Hombre," I said, "the kids are going to be electrocuted."

"Na! Nunca! - These are modern times we're living in. They've got to get used to that sort of thing!"

The same wires are still dangling there. It still sparks across the street when it rains! No one has ever been hurt. I suppose they are all good Catholics!

We have had four different alcaldes in the village since we have lived here, and each one in turn, in the course of conversation has said to me - and I quote:

"Fran', por Navidad segtuo viene la electricidad hasta su casa!" - For Christmas you'll have electricity for sure! We still haven't got it, but three years ago we installed solar lighting. The young man who fitted it lives about thirty miles away in a village called Sierra de Yeguas - Mountain of the Mares! What a lovely name. He mentioned the fact that his wife, Inmaculada, ran the infants' school in his *pueblo* - if he came on Sunday to finish the job, could he bring her along as it was the only day that they could be together?

"Of course, come to lunch and bring the kids," said Sylvia, delighted at the thought.

On Sunday morning they trundled up in his clapped-out old car, the boot loaded down with plaques, battery, coils of wire, dolls, comics, tools etc. They are a delightful family! Inma is a lovely, sparkling, typical Andaluz - she bubbled! Sylvia showed her around the house. She oohed and aahed over my paintings and sculptures, and gasped at all the books stowed in all odd corners. The kids rolled on the floor and played with the kittens whilst Antonio and I carried on with the work - me doing the labouring. He said that ours was the sort of house he really would have liked to live in, but, owing to his business, he had to be in a more civilized town. However, seven years previously they had bought a big old house in Sierra, the ground floor being used as his workshop. They had nearly finished the two upper floors using old materials. In the school buildings his wife had spent her time scraping doors, painting, scrounging old furniture etc. and it was now practically finished - and would we come and stay with them for Christmas? Just like that!

Later that afternoon, Nuria, their small daughter aged

about three and a half, said to her parents, "Papa - Mama - I've got a new abuelita!" (little grandmother).

"Who is this then, niña?"

"Sylvia," said Nuria proudly, taking my wife by the hand.

"Well," said Antonio turning to me. "Then you must be my Papa!"

He turned, gave me an *abrazo*, kissed me on both cheeks and stood back with a big smile on his face. I felt a mixture of emotions. Coming all over Anglo-Saxon, I was embarrassed, astonished, pleased, and quite at a loss! Sylvia was delighted! She kissed the kids, Mario, the boy aged seven blushed then kissed her back. Inma kissed her - then me - I liked that! And by this time I had regained my cool, stopped, and thought - "What a lovely, warm, spontaneous gesture!" Two older people, complete strangers, foreigners in their land, are accepted at face value just because the youngsters liked us.

It was astonishing and very warming and rather humbling. The last time we had been to England we nipped into the Waterloo station restaurant for a quick cup of tea. When the woman behind the counter handed it to me, I said without really thinking, "Muchas gracias." "Oh Christ," said the lady, "another bloody Spaniard!"

Chapter 39

One Sunday morning I was cutting the grass around the big date-palm that grows in front of the house. I had tried keeping the ground cleared as we used it for parking the car, but it was a 'Forth Bridge' job - the weeds grew as fast as I dug them, so in desperation I tried the old lawn mower and now, if one doesn't look too closely, it could be called a lawn, sort of. Anyway, that morning I had stopped to light my pipe when a voice behind me said, "Hola, Fran - como estas?"

I turned - it was young Diego who had come down from the village to collect wild asparagus for his mum. It grows on the Mountainside in front of us. "Hola, chico," I said. "That's a fair bunch of asparagus you have there - Mama will be very pleased."

"Sí," - he nodded. Then pointing to the lawnmower said, "What is that machine? What is it for?"

"Oh, it's used for cutting the grass."

"Sí! - Why?"

"Well - I - er," thinking quickly - "it's - er - to make it took nice - er - the garden," I said lamely. "Grass? Sí?"

He shook his head. No countryman here ever cuts grass unless he wants it for animal feed. "Que curioso!" said the lad. All foreigners are rather odd, as everyone knows, and he was too polite to say he thought I was potty. "How does it work then?"

I gave it a push around the palm tree - grass flew in all

directions. He nodded his head, looked at me, then walked away slowly down the drive. "Que curioso, que curioso," he was saying to himself. I don't suppose there has ever been a lawnmower within thirty miles of Carratraca - no wonder he thought it *curioso*!

Chapter 40

In the course of her work as a journalist Sylvia had to cover the Wedding of the Year, the bride being the niece of Prince Hohenlohe, the founder of the Marbella Club and Numero Uno of the Costa del Sol jet-set. The bridegroom was the second son of the Duchess of Alba, the most prestigious landowner in Spain. Sylvia has met the Prince many times, and has a great respect for him and for what he has done for tourism in Andalucia. His new urbanization is built over a Roman bridge and accordingly is called Puente Romano, but the restaurant in which the reception was to be held was just on the point of being finished and at that period was a big empty area with bare, whitewashed walls, facing the tropical gardens.

"You have only two or three days before the wedding," said Sylvia. "How are you going to decorate the place in time?"

"I really don't know," said the Prince. "A few palm leaves, I suppose - and some flowers here and there - I don't really know."

"That's going to be rather a let-down! Tell you what! Frank has a lot of sculptures at home in the Molino. He doesn't want to sell them as he is trying to get enough work done to hold an exhibition - but I'm sure he would be willing to lend them to you for the wedding - if you think them suitable. I have some photos of them in the car."

The upshot was that he asked for them all - plus San

Francisco. The wedding over, we went down, but Saint Francis wasn't there. "No," said Prince Alfonso - "because I want him for my gardens - and so does my architect! How much will your husband take for him?"

"He belongs to me," said my wife - "and he lives on the rock in front of my house! I don't want to sell him - so there!"

"Sylvia! You have the sculptor and lots of fig trees - and you can get another Santo! I will give you what you ask for him. I want him for my gardens. Name a price!"

"Right," said Sylvia - "one thousand pounds and a pair of those white doves you have in your church tower!"

"Done!" said Prince Alfonso - and smiled.

"Gracias," said Sylvia - and looked all smug.

"Jeesus!" said Paco Norte - and promptly fainted!

This windfall paid for the finishing-off of El Molino and tiled completely the now finished ground floor.

Chapter 41

Sylvia is a cataholic. She can spot a feline thirty yards away, make suitable pussycat noises and, six to four, it will come over and rub itself against her leg. We hadn't been long at the Molino when a tiny ginger kitten arrived from goodness knows where. It was pampered and fussed over as though it was the only one left. Eventually, of course, it became a cat - this happens. We called her Marmalady until - things being as is - we had to call her Marmaduke. As he grew older he would disappear for two or three days at a time and the valley would echo to "Marmy - Marmy! Milky - Milky!" Of course he always came back, he was onto a good thing, and he knew it!

Came the day when he arrived back with a popsey - a tiny white tabby with ginger spots. But dear, oh dear, what a pathetic little thing she was, thin, dirty and very hungry. We said, "Is that the best you can do, Marmy?" But he thought she was smashing. She stopped at the doorway. "Come on," said his Lordship, "you'll be all right as long as you're with me - this is my house - these humans belong to me. All you have to do is lean up against the leg of the smaller one, and purr. Come on, you'll see." She did as he suggested and was rewarded with a saucer of milk and an egg. Then some pieces of fish which she shared with her feller, "'Cos of course he must be hungry too, poor old Marmy!" He was, but not just for fish.

Within a couple of weeks, Snowdrop, as she was now

called, was sleek and fat and beautiful, and doing all the ordering about, with Marmaduke taking second place - as ever was! Two or three weeks elapsed and then sex reared its ugly head in the Valley of the Canes! It was rather a shame Milord hadn't had any instruction in that sort of thing - no Farver - no Muvver, and he made a right old mess of it! (I was going to say a right old cock of it but he obviously didn't.) Of all places he would insist on practising on the big rock in front of the house which has a slope of thirty degrees, and the more he pushed, the faster she slid down the rock. (I suggested that I go and help him but I was called a dirty old man! - I'm not old!) He was only practising obviously, because if Sylvia shouted "Fishy-fishy," they immediately packed up and went inside to eat. I only hope I never get as hungry as that!

Eventually, of course, she became 'preggy' - it had to be, but when her time came along she was really in distress and mewed piteously. Sylvia knelt down by the side of her box, stroked her gently then laid her hands on the swollen body. Snowdrop quietened, lay still for a while, and then with an effort ejected three dead kittens one after the other, showing then, for the first time, her affection by gratefully licking Sylvia's hands and purring. From then on she has given birth regularly twice a year and Carratraca has more ginger kittens per metre than any other *pueblo* in Andalucia. Cats in the *campo* do not have a long life as a rule. Apart from trigger-happy Spanish hunters - who will shoot at anything that can run, walk, wriggle, swim or fly, they have too many natural enemies. Foxes, lynxes, farm dogs, civets all take their toll, but their most dangerous opponents seem to be domestic cats that have 'gone bust'. These animals have had to be tough to survive and will attack domestic cats for their food or for mating. House cats don't stand a chance. At the time of writing there is a big thick-coated mountain tom who visits us when he feels like a bit of 'nooky', - bangs all our Tabbies one after the other and claws any young mates to pieces. I would shoot him but I haven't got a gun - I don't expect I could kill him anyway. Old Raphael says "poison him", but that's very nasty and I jib at that. He even came into the house one day - saucy sod! I managed to hit him with the hoe I had in my hand but his fur is so thick it just bounced off him, and he shot up the chimney and over the roof-top. A few nights later I caught him in the beam of my headlights sitting on the bridge. "Got you - you bastard!" I said, put my foot on the accelerator - and sounded my horn! Silly old me! Ah well, I might have missed him anyway.

Then we had an 'outside cat' - as distinct from Marmy and Snowdrop who were 'inside cats' - and she disappeared! Pandemonium! Where was Sooty? Oh dear! Sylvia had resigned herself to the loss, when about a month later she appeared proudly around the corner of my workshop with a tiny painted kitten in tow. My wife was delighted - "Sooty! Sooty! Oh, and look at her baby - we'll call her Pinta!" They were just drinking a second saucer of milk when another little black and white kitten appeared. "Look look! Another little Poppet!" said the Boss. "We'll name her Niña - it must be a little female - more milk!" Ten minutes later a white one trotted up with its little tail stuck up in the air. I know - it had to be - it's Santa Maria!

Santa, when still only a kitten, fell thirty feet off the roof down into the mill 'ole. Poor little sausage! She mewed piteously all night but we didn't find her until the following morning. I think it must have stunted her growth as she is the smallest cat we've ever had.

Santa Maria lived for many years and stayed on as an outside cat at El Molino. At about five years old she reappeared after a twelve-day absence with a desiccated foreleg which having dried in a trap permitted her to hobble back to us. With no vet nearer than the coast, Sylvia 'operated'. Within twenty-four hours Santa was walking on those three legs, along with the cane support for vines! As fit as before! A miracle! (What the village heard about traps from my Missus stood the cats in good stead for about fifteen years.)

Tina, our little cocker bitch, you know - couldn't tell puppies from kitties and would suckle any of them quite happily.

Anyway, if ever you have forty-eight hours to spare, come along and Sylvia will show you her photos of cats!